Women in Literature

BY ALEXIS BURLING

CONTENT CONSULTANT
Donna M. Decker, PhD
Professor, English Department
Franklin Pierce University, Rindge, New Hampshire

Essential Library

An Imprint of Abdo Publishing | abdopublishing.com

WOMEN'S LIVES *in* Hi*story*

abdopublishing.com

Published by Abdo Publishing, a division of ABDO, PO Box 398166, Minneapolis, Minnesota 55439. Copyright © 2017 by Abdo Consulting Group, Inc. International copyrights reserved in all countries. No part of this book may be reproduced in any form without written permission from the publisher. Essential Library™ is a trademark and logo of Abdo Publishing.

Printed in the United States of America, North Mankato, Minnesota
052016
092016

 THIS BOOK CONTAINS
RECYCLED MATERIALS

Cover Photo: Shutterstock Images
Interior Photos: Tim Sloan/AFP/Getty Images, 4–5; AP Images, 8, 14–15, 16–17, 47, 72; David Goldman/AP Images, 9; Harris & Ewing/Library of Congress, 11, 58; Beowulf Sheehan/Corbis, 13; John Amis/AP Images, 20; Peter Morrison/AP Images, 22; Writer Pictures/Geraint Lewis/AP Images, 23; sergeyryzhov/iStockphoto/Thinkstock, 24–25; Library of Congress, 27, 59, 64–65; Richard Drew/AP Images, 29; Bettmann/Corbis, 31, 40; Edi Engeler/Keystone/AP Images, 33; North Wind Picture Archives, 34–35; ABC/Photofest, 39; Barry Brecheisen/Invision/AP Images, 43; Steven Senne/AP Images, 44–45; Rebecca Sapp/WireImage/Getty Images, 49; Rob Latour/Rex Features/AP Images, 52; George Grantham Bain Collection/Library of Congress, 54–55; Fred Palumbo/New York World-Telegram and the Sun Newspaper Photograph Collection/Library of Congress, 57; Jim Wells/AP Images, 62; Bill Chaplis/AP Images, 68; Ozier Muhammad/Ebony Collection/AP Images, 70; Warren K. Leffler/Library of Congress, 71; Katy Winn/Corbis, 75; Clark Jones/Courtesy of Scholastic, Inc./AP Images, 76–77; Red Line Editorial, 80–81; Katy Winn/AP Images, 83; Summit Entertainment/Photofest, 84; David Massey/AP Images, 86–87; Matt Sayles/Invision for PEN Center USA/AP Images, 88–89; Keith Srakocic/AP Images, 91; Denis Poroy/Invision/AP Images, 93; Lynn Goldsmith/Corbis, 96–97

Editor: Mari Kesselring
Series Designer: Maggie Villaume

Cataloging-in-Publication Data
Names: Burling, Alexis, author.
Title: Women in literature / by Alexis Burling.
Description: Minneapolis, MN : Abdo Publishing, [2017] | Series: Women's lives
    in history | Includes bibliographical references and index.
Identifiers: LCCN 2015960355 | ISBN 9781680782929 (lib. bdg.) |
    ISBN 9781680774863 (ebook)
Subjects: LCSH: Literature--Women authors--Juvenile literature. | Women in the
    professions--Juvenile literature.
Classification: DDC 800--dc23
LC record available at http://lccn.loc.gov/2015960355

Contents

Maya Angelou received the
Medal of Freedom from
President Obama.

CHAPTER ONE

Dr. Maya Angelou: Legendary Poet

On February 15, 2011, a hush moved through the crowd gathered in the East Room of the White House as President Barack Obama entered. Wearing a dark suit, pressed white shirt, and striped navy tie, he walked to the podium and stood. Cameras flashed, and reporters, White House staffers, and dignitaries took their seats.

"This is one of the things that I most look forward to every year. It's a chance to meet with—and, more importantly, honor—some of the most extraordinary people in America—and around the world," the president said, looking out into the room. "This year's Medal of Freedom recipients reveal the best of who we are and who we aspire to be."[1]

After reading the first name and presenting a medal, Obama fixed his gaze on a stately woman in a black velvet-and-satin dress, seated to his right. As an announcer read the honorarium aloud, Obama placed the gold Medal of Freedom—the country's highest civilian honor—around the woman's neck.

> "One isn't necessarily born with courage, but one is born with potential. Without courage, we cannot practice any other virtue with consistency. We can't be kind, true, merciful, generous, or honest."[3]
>
> —*Maya Angelou*

"Out of a youth marked by pain and injustice, Dr. Maya Angelou rose with an unbending determination to fight for civil rights and inspire every one of us to recognize and embrace the possibility and potential we each hold," the announcer said. "With her soaring poetry, towering prose, and mastery of a range of art forms, Dr. Angelou has spoken to the conscience of our nation. Her soul-stirring words have taught us how to reach across division and honor the beauty of our world."[2]

A Pioneer of Firsts

During her 86 years, Maya Angelou was one of the most talented writers of our time. Before her death in 2014, she wrote more than ten volumes of poetry, including the Pulitzer Prize–nominated collection *Just Give Me a Cool Drink of Water 'Fore I Diiie*. She authored dozens of scripts for plays and television programs, songs for musicals and films, and cookbooks filled with her favorite Southern recipes. She even wrote a number of books for children, including *Life Doesn't Frighten Me*. Her spoken-word albums, "On the Pulse of Morning," "Phenomenal Woman," and "A Song Flung Up to Heaven," earned her three Grammys.

But Angelou is perhaps best known for the seven memoirs she wrote about her life. Born on April 4, 1928, in Saint Louis, Missouri, Angelou was one of the first authors to take her experiences as an African-American female and turn them into bare-all autobiographies. Angelou grew up in the Jim Crow South when blacks were segregated from whites and had virtually no rights. Her memoirs serve as permanent reminders to the world that living as an African American and as a woman in the United States in the mid-1900s was no easy feat.

Angelou's first memoir, *I Know Why the Caged Bird Sings*, details Angelou's difficult childhood in rural Stamps, Arkansas, through the birth of her son when she was 17. The book includes graphic descriptions of a rape by one of her mother's boyfriends. It also touches on his subsequent murder—a traumatic event that caused Maya to stop speaking from the time she was

MORE THAN AN AUTHOR

In addition to her literary accomplishments, Angelou achieved great success in many other areas. As a teenager, she became the first African-American female streetcar conductor in San Francisco, California. As a performer in the 1950s, she toured 22 countries with a US State Department production of the opera *Porgy and Bess* and produced an album of songs called *Miss Calypso*. As a civil rights activist, Angelou worked alongside Dr. Martin Luther King Jr. and Malcolm X in the 1960s. She served on two presidential committees, for Gerald Ford in 1975 and for Jimmy Carter in 1977. And in 1981, she was appointed a lifetime faculty member at Wake Forest University in Winston-Salem, North Carolina. She received more than 50 honorary degrees in her lifetime.

Angelou summed up her attitude on success in a speech she gave in 1990 to students at Centenary College in Louisiana. She said, "See me now, black, female, American, and southern. See me and see yourselves. What can't you do?"[4]

Angelou posed with her breakthrough publication *I Know Why the Caged Bird Sings* in 1971.

seven until she turned 12. At the time of the book's publication, the depiction of violence surprised some American readers who were not accustomed to such blunt honesty in women's literature.

Published in 1969, *I Know Why the Caged Bird Sings* made literary history. It became the first nonfiction best seller by an African-American woman. It is now required reading in many high schools and universities across the country, has been translated into more than 17 languages, and has sold more than one million copies worldwide.

Because of her gender and race, Angelou faced challenges for most of her life. But despite the frequent prejudice she encountered, Angelou refused to let anyone get in the way of her dreams or thwart her accomplishments—especially when it

Angelou wrote many books, including several best sellers.

came to writing. In poems such as "Phenomenal Woman," she celebrated the strength and beauty of womanhood. In her essays, she argued for equal rights for all humankind, no matter what race, creed, color, or sex. And in her memoirs, she exposed compelling but often painful truths about her

MAYA ANGELOU IN SPACE

Angelou and her work have been honored many times in different ways. In December 2014, several months after Angelou's death, NASA's Orion spacecraft hurtled more than 3,600 miles (5,800 km) into outer space. The trip was supposed to test the spacecraft's safety systems before it could begin shuttling astronauts to far-off wonders in the solar system. Packed inside tiny lockers within the spacecraft were several of Angelou's poems, as well as excerpts from some of her books.

During an awards ceremony held on April 6, 2015, NASA Administrator Charles Bolden explained why NASA had chosen Angelou's works to accompany Orion. "It is fitting that Maya Angelou's prophetic words be flown not only outside the bounds of our Earth, but on the maiden voyage of a spacecraft that represents humanity's aspirations to move beyond our planet, to reach higher, and become more than we have ever been," said Bolden.[5]

life—such as financial setbacks and single motherhood—to inspire other women to rise above the limitations society imposed on them.

Women Writers: A Giant Leap

For centuries, women writers of all races and colors have confronted hurdles. Some were confined by the social expectation that they devote their energy to their children and husbands rather than their own endeavors. As a result, they had less time to produce work and published far less than their male counterparts. Other women found their writing was valued less simply because they were female. Some took to writing under male pseudonyms to appease publishers and reach a wider audience of readers who still weren't comfortable with the idea of women writing notable works. Still others never got published at all.

But despite these obstacles, female visionaries, including Angelou, have altered the literary landscape. They have demanded that their voices be heard on their terms. They have used their

Women hold their awards from a 1924 writing contest. There were few opportunities for female authors during this time.

ANGELOU'S WORK LIVES ON

Angelou died on May 28, 2014, at her longtime home in Winston-Salem, North Carolina. But the work she did throughout her life inspired the literary careers of many other women, including Alice Walker, Toni Morrison, Nikki Giovanni, Jamaica Kincaid, Gwendolyn Brooks, and others. One such author was Nikky Finney. When Finney won the 2011 National Book Award for Poetry, she said Angelou was "a mountain of a human being. . . . Hers was a story for us all. She was proudly African American, but she was passionately human."[6]

experiences and beliefs to not only shape the content of their writing but also to define how works written by women are perceived. Now, the list of accomplished female writers is long and varied. Madeleine L'Engle started writing science fiction during the 1950s when authors of the genre were mostly men. Her struggle to be recognized paid off when she received the prestigious Newbery Medal in 1963 for her novel *A Wrinkle in Time*. Judy Blume set the stage for what would become a worldwide phenomenon: young adult fiction. Her groundbreaking 1970 novel *Are You There God? It's Me, Margaret* was so honest about the then-unmentionable topic of puberty that it caught the attention of millions of young readers.

Women of color have made vital advancements in the literary world too. Mexican-American essayist and short story writer Sandra Cisneros was the first female Hispanic author to get a publishing contract by a major US publishing house for *Woman Hollering Creek and Other Stories*. She was also one of the first Latina writers to win the prestigious MacArthur "Genius Grant" Fellowship in 1995. This grant of $625,000 is given to 20 to 30 writers, visual artists, and thinkers each year. Jacqueline Woodson is another trailblazer. Her poetry, like Angelou's, has received the highest praise for its willingness to confront race and gender issues head on. Her memoir, *Brown Girl Dreaming,* won the National Book Award for Young People's Literature in 2014.

Many phenomenal literary women have helped define the course of history. Whether in fiction or nonfiction, poetry or graphic novels, outspoken women such as Betty Friedan, Alice Walker, Ursula K. Le Guin, and Maxine Hong Kingston pushed boundaries. They fought against narrow-mindedness and pioneered new, revolutionary ways of thinking. And they did so by producing cutting-edge works of literary art.

Angelou blazed the trail for authors including Jacqueline Woodson, who was honored with a National Book Award in 2014.

Willa Cather is known as a pioneer in literary fiction.

CHAPTER TWO

Literary Fiction

Before she died on April 24, 1947, author Willa Cather was not a celebrity in today's sense of the word. The rural Virginia and Nebraska native was reserved. She often turned down interviews. She forbade members of the press to print quotes from her letters in their newspapers. Yet some historians view Cather as one of the most accomplished writers of her time.

Cather began her writing career as a journalist in Pittsburgh, Pennsylvania, in 1896 at the age of 22. In 1906, she moved to New York, where she was the managing editor of *McClure's*, a news and literary magazine. But Cather is best known for her fiction recounting the grueling daily lives of frontier Americans. Women during Cather's time were encouraged to marry and spend their lives caring for their children rather than having careers. But Cather never married or had children. Instead, she spent most of her time writing. She penned 12 novels during her lifetime, including the 1923 Pulitzer Prize–winning *One of Ours* and the popular *My Ántonia*. Critic H. L. Mencken

said of the work, "No romantic novel ever written in America, by man or woman, is one half so beautiful as *My Ántonia*."[1]

Cather was considered a talented writer of literary fiction. Literary fiction is a type of storytelling that attempts to explore the human condition over time. It often contains an overarching theme. Over the course of the next century, many more gifted literary fiction writers entered the scene. Authors such as Ayn Rand, Doris Lessing, Toni Morrison, and Alice Walker took the most pressing issues of the day—civil rights, the oppression of women, economic inequality in urban areas, religion—and transformed them into literary fiction. These were stories the public could understand and learn from. With the power of their words, these women captured the public's imagination. They made history—and the human experience—meaningful.

CATHER'S PRIVATE LIFE

Despite Cather's wish for her letters to be kept from the public eye, a volume containing many of them was published in 2013, long after the author's death. A number of secrets came to light, including the much-speculated fact that Cather might have been a lesbian. She lived for 38 years in domestic partnership with a woman named Edith Lewis in New York City. Thought to be the love of Cather's life, Lewis also edited the author's writing.

Talking Politics

One of the aims of literary fiction is to deliver an entertaining story to readers. But the genre also has other motives. Many twentieth-century authors of literary fiction

were influenced by political movements. They wanted to bring about change in their own lives and in society at large. Russian-born Ayn Rand was perhaps one of the most subversive novelists writing during the 1940s and 1950s. Her work promoted a strict form of capitalism and praised reason and individualism over compassion. But many critics disliked it. Still, Rand's best-known novels, *The Fountainhead* and the 1,200-page dystopian allegory *Atlas Shrugged*, gained a cult following that persists to this day. They continue to sell nearly 800,000 books a year more than 30 years after the author's death in 1982.[2]

Many female authors have used literary fiction to advocate for the rights of women. In the 1960s, the concept of feminism was becoming popular in the United States. At that time, most women were expected to focus on family life. They had few opportunities to work and learn outside the home.

Doris Lessing was one author who used her writing to push for greater freedoms for women and promote feminism. Lessing's novel *The Golden Notebook* was called the "handbook of feminism" when it was published in 1962. The book tells the story of a female writer's struggles to reconcile her professional aspirations with her

"I COULDN'T CARE LESS."

Throughout her life, Lessing was always a free thinker. Sometimes this got her in trouble. She lived all over the world, from a childhood in Persia (now Iran) and Southern Rhodesia (now Zimbabwe) to an adulthood spent in London, England.

During her years of writing she dabbled in communism, protested racist practices in Zimbabwe, and spoke out for women's rights. She also had a husband and two children but left them to pursue her career. "I couldn't stand that life," Lessing said in an interview. "It's this business of giving all the time, day and night, trying to conform to something you hate."[3]

In 2007, Lessing won the Nobel Prize for Literature. When a journalist arrived at her door to tell her the news, she responded, "I couldn't care less."[4]

increasingly restrictive duties as a mother. "[*The Golden Notebook*] was daring in its day for its frank exploration of the inner lives of women who, unencumbered by marriage, were free to raise children, or not, and pursue work and their sex lives as they chose," wrote *New York Times* journalist Helen Verongos.[5]

Literary Icons

Literary fiction provides an avenue for many types of social change. Two of the most influential literary authors of the 1900s are Alice Walker and Toni Morrison. Working during the civil rights era of the 1960s and 1970s, the two African-American authors shattered many barriers and earned great honors for their work.

Throughout Walker's storied career, the media and her devoted fans have championed her for using her writing to challenge both racism and sexism. Walker writes candidly about issues facing women, including abortion and domestic violence. She has written novels, volumes of poetry, collections of short stories, and many essays speaking out for the marginalized and the poor around the globe. Her 1982 novel, *The Color Purple,* was made into an Oscar-nominated film and won the National Book Award and the Pulitzer Prize. This was the first Pulitzer Prize for Fiction win for an African-American woman.

Toni Morrison also stands out as a giant in the field of literary fiction. She has garnered praise for her body of work, which chronicles the African-American experience. Many of her works critique America's treatment of blacks throughout history and focus on the lives of black women. Her first

Walker used her literary fiction to combat racism and sexism in society.

novel, *The Bluest Eye,* was published in 1970. It tells the story of an African-American girl who believes her life would be better if she had blue eyes. Morrison's 1988 novel, *Beloved,* features the shocking story of a runaway slave who cuts her daughter's throat rather than relinquish her to a former slave owner. Morrison's work addresses some of the darkest yet truthful themes in American literature.

Morrison's influence on contemporary literature is vast. In 1988, *Beloved* was awarded the Pulitzer Prize. She won the Nobel Prize in 1993—a first for African-American women. Through both her success and her writing, she has elevated the status of female authors of color within the world of literary fiction.

New Talent

In today's publishing world, talented female literary fiction writers abound—each making great strides in subject and form and paving the way for even more strong female authors. Chilean-American writer Isabel Allende uses magical realism. This literary style combines realistic fiction with fantastical elements. Allende uses magical realism to make sense of turbulent moments in history in novels such as *The House of Spirits* and *The Japanese Lover*. In *The House of Spirits*, she sets the story of three generations of the Trueba family against the backdrop of an unnamed Latin American country's peaceful socialist revolution and violent counterrevolution. *The Japanese Lover* addresses the horrors of Nazi occupation during World War II (1939–1945), the internment of Japanese Americans, and the AIDS epidemic. Her books have sold 65 million copies worldwide. In 2014, when she was 72, she received the Presidential Medal of Freedom.

Many works of literary fiction are short stories. Female authors, such as Lorrie Moore and Alice Munro, have excelled in this area. With more than a dozen story collections to her credit, Munro has made a name for herself chronicling the tangled relationships between men and women. She became the thirteenth woman to win the Nobel Prize in Literature in 2013. She was 82 years old.

Munro reads from one of her collections at a press conference at Trinity College in Dublin, Ireland.

Moore's signature wit has earned her the praise of critics and a following of pun-obsessed fans. "Moore is notable for her arch tone and her sharp humor," wrote critic Elizabeth Day in the *Guardian*.[6]

Whether it's Nigerian writer Chimamanda Ngozi Adichie, who heralded a new generation of African authors with her essay *We Should All Be Feminists* in 2014, or 28-year-old New Zealander Eleanor Catton, who became the youngest woman to win the Man Booker Prize in 2013 for her novel *The Luminaries*, there are many new literary stars on the horizon. While many women writers have achieved recognition for their work in literary fiction, there are always new frontiers to be explored.

Chimamanda Ngozi Adichie

Chimamanda Ngozi Adichie was born and raised in Nigeria. When she was 19 years old, she traveled to the United States for college. She published her first novel, *Purple Hibiscus*, in 2003.

In 2006, Adichie published the luminous novel *Half of a Yellow Sun*. In it, she relayed the story of three lives torn apart by war in 1960s Nigeria. After the novel was published, it won the Baileys Woman's Prize for Fiction. Author and journalist Muriel Gray, who chaired the judging panel in 2007, said of Adichie, "For an author, so young at the time of writing, to have been able to tell a tale of such enormous scale in terms of human suffering and the consequences of hatred and division . . . is an astonishing feat."[7]

Since then, Adichie has impressed readers and critics alike with her short story collection *The Thing Around Your Neck*. Her third novel, *Americanah*, which follows two lovers facing starkly different realities before they reunite in Nigeria—one in post-9/11 America and the other in London—provides a nuanced commentary on race and identity.

(1977–)

Genre fiction is one of the highest-selling categories of books.

CHAPTER THREE

Genre Fiction

Supermarkets and bookstores all over the United States have book aisles with rows of paperback books, mostly of the same shape and size. Some might have two covers, each with a different alluring image of two lovers intertwined and a cutout in the middle. Others might feature a detective casing a crime scene. Each year, these types of books sell by the millions. They belong to a subset of literature referred to as genre fiction.

Genre fiction—also called popular or mass-market fiction—is plot-heavy and action-driven fiction that is written to match a particular literary category. Two of the most widely read categories of genre fiction are romance and mystery. In 2013, sales of romance novels captured 13 percent of the adult fiction market, totaling $1.08 billion.

Readers of both sexes love mass-market books. But over the last 100 years, women have been writing them too. If it weren't for women writers such as Jackie Collins, Kathleen E. Woodiwiss, Nora Roberts, and Beverly Jenkins, romance sections in bookstores and online would look a lot less crowded than they do today.

Love Is in the Air

Stories full of romance and courtship have been popular for centuries. But in the early 1800s, author Jane Austen published a series of six novels, starting with *Sense and Sensibility*, that were groundbreaking. Austen's books are still some of the most widely read love stories. Unlike in other genres, such as nonfiction and science fiction, where men have mostly dominated the writing landscape for the past century, female authors have had an easier time getting published in the romance genre. Many publishers consider women authorities on subjects such as love and domestic matters. Since writing romance does not necessarily challenge any gendered traditions, it is sometimes seen as a more acceptable topic for women to write about.

But just because female writers excel at publishing romance novels doesn't mean they do not push barriers. Two of the first female novelists to turn up the heat and revamp romance publishing into something racier were Jackie Collins and Kathleen E. Woodiwiss. Prior to the late 1960s, most romances that made it into readers' hands had much of the action happening off the page. But in their steamy debut novels, Collins and Woodiwiss both openly describe sex using intentionally graphic prose. "[Jackie Collins's] motto was girls can do anything. And that didn't just apply to sexual empowerment," said freelance journalist Annalisa Quinn on National Public Radio. "Her heroines are fearless, and women find that empowering."[1]

Jane Austen

(1775–1817)

Jane Austen was born on December 16, 1775, in Steventon, Hampshire, England. Her family's home contained a vast library for Jane and her siblings to use. Few young women during this time had such free access to books.

Austen wrote stories and plays as a young teenager, including a series of love letters later published under the title *Lady Susan*. But it wasn't until she was in her thirties that she attempted to publish her fiction—writing anonymously as "a Lady."

From 1811 to 1815, Austen published *Sense and Sensibility, Pride and Prejudice, Mansfield Park,* and *Emma.* All were hugely successful. But her readers did not know she wrote them. After her death in 1817, Austen's brother Henry revealed to the public that Jane was the author of the books. Today, Austen's romances are some of the most widely read books in history.

In the 1960s and 1970s, Collins and Woodiwiss's books were banned in conservative places such as South Africa and China, where women's freedoms were more limited. But the books were huge hits in increasingly progressive countries such as the United States.

A NEW FACE IN HISTORICAL ROMANCE

Historical romance is the most popular subset of the billion-dollar romance publishing industry. Many of the covers feature women with long blonde hair and flowing gowns, with large estates behind them. But African-American history is rarely included.

Romance writer Beverly Jenkins was determined to set readers—and publishers—straight. When she was first starting out in 1994, the reception toward romance writers of color was bleak. She faced pushback for her first book, *Night Song.* Jenkins remembered, "[Publishers] didn't have a box for it."[2]

But since then, people—especially fans and other romance writers—have started to change. Because of Jenkins, they're both reading—and writing—books featuring protagonists of color with multicultural backgrounds. "She's paved the way," said romance author Piper Huguley in 2015. "[She let] people know that there is an audience out there that's hungry to read a different kind of historical, an American story, featuring American people."[3]

From that point forward, romance writers were free to concoct any type of situation imaginable. As women in society began to be seen not just as housewives but also as equal partners in love and romance, the content of romance novels shifted. Writers such as Danielle Steel and Jude Deveraux, whose books feature headstrong and independent female protagonists with jobs, strong opinions, and a sense of self-worth, became enormously popular. Nora Roberts did too, penning more than 200 erotic novels since 1981. By 2014, there were more than 500 million copies of Roberts's books in print.

New romance writers have seen massive successes in recent years too, attracting all types of readers. But the racial makeup of the genre is still quite narrow. The vast majority of romance writers are white—and so are their characters. Some publishers have begun to establish separate imprints for books written by nonwhite authors featuring nonwhite protagonists. But many authors, such as Beverly Jenkins, think it's still not enough. "People say, 'Well, I can't relate,'" said Jenkins, who is African American. "But you can relate to shapeshifters, you can relate to vampires, you can relate to werewolves, but you can't relate to a story written by and about black Americans? I got a problem with that."[4]

Steel's romance novels feature strong female characters.

M Is for Mystery

Despite the need for more diversity in the genre, female romance writers saw success throughout much of the 1900s. But detective novels and mysteries written by women were much less common. Overshadowed by the sheer volume of books published by noir or crime fiction giants such as Dashiell Hammett, Raymond Chandler, and Mickey Spillane, women's work in the genre was largely ignored. Because of the sometimes gruesome subject matter and the history of masculine protagonists as the genre developed, women were not considered the primary creators or readers of the genre. But one writer was instrumental in proving that women could indeed write fascinating mysteries: British author Agatha Christie.

Christie was highly productive during what is considered the golden age of mystery novels, the period between World War I and World War II (1918–1939). She adopted the typical characteristics of the mystery genre: an eccentric but supremely logical detective, plenty of mini cliffhangers, and

THE FIRST FEMALE-WRITTEN DETECTIVE NOVEL

The first woman to publish a detective novel in America was Anna Katherine Green. Her book, *The Leavenworth Case*, was published in 1878. After the book about an infamous murder and subsequent legal case was released, the public became obsessed with the exploits of detective Ebenezer Gryce, who appears in some of Green's subsequent novels. Some historians classify the book as one of this country's first best sellers. *The Leavenworth Case* sold three-quarters of a million copies over a 15-year period—a whopping amount at that time. Green did such a good job in depicting the courtroom scenes that her book was later used in Yale University law classes as an example of the pitfalls of trusting inconclusive evidence.

Christie was a trailblazer for women writing mysteries.

BARBARA NEELY: CHANGING PERCEPTIONS

Barbara Neely has lived a storied life. She has worked as a radio talk-show host, a political activist, and has designed a correctional facility. She is also a groundbreaking writer of mysteries.

Her mysteries star Blanche White, an African-American housemaid turned amateur investigator. *Blanche* is the French word for "white." Neely named her protagonist White White on purpose. She wanted readers to think about race, class, and gender issues when reading her fiction.

challenging the reader to guess the culprit by the end of the book. But she also created a campy style uniquely her own. Unlike popular mysteries of the day, Christie's detectives often avoided violence. Some even used gags, such as a soap-squirt in the eye, to stop a murderer from getting away.

During her lifetime, Christie penned 78 crime novels, 19 plays, 6 romantic novels using the name Mary Westmacott, and 4 nonfiction books, including an autobiography. Two of her most famous novels are *And Then There Were None* and *Murder on the Orient Express*. In 2010, sales of her books reached more than 2 billion copies worldwide.[5] According to some estimates, Christie is the world's second-most translated author and one of the most widely read writers in history.

Though no other mystery writer—male or female—has been as successful as Christie in the last 100 years, a number of other women have made their mark on the genre. Award winner Patricia Highsmith's dark suspense novels and short story collections—including her first book, *Strangers on a Train,* published in 1950—were beloved by millions of fans for their ingenious plot twists, handsome but detestable villains, and electrifying prose. Canadian author Margaret Millar wrote most of her

"No use asking if a crime writer has anything of the criminal in him. He perpetuates little hoaxes, lies and crimes every time he writes a book."

7. Die Gesellschaft als Gefängnis oder Die universelle Observation

A 2006 exhibition in Berne, Switzerland, honored the work of Patricia Highsmith, who spent some of her life in southern Switzerland.

21 mystery novels when she was legally blind. Recognized for penning best-selling psychological thrillers, Millar was voted Woman of the Year by the *Los Angeles Times* in 1965.

Other female mystery writers worked to introduce more diversity into the genre and its authors. Writer Barbara Neely was determined to change the prevailing perception that all good mysteries were written by and about white men. Her award-winning books starring Blanche White, a middle-aged African-American housekeeper turned amateur detective, filled a hole in the mystery-publishing world in the early 1990s. "Neely blazed a trail for other women and minority crime novelists," said Joel Goldman, Neely's publisher and founder of Brash Books. "She gives a voice to a character who was previously invisible."[6]

Mary Shelley wrote
Frankenstein, one of the most
famous science fiction novels.

Science Fiction

I n the preface to the 1831 edition of Mary Shelley's enduring classic *Frankenstein*, the author explains that the idea for the chill-inducing novel came to her in a nightmare. Shelley wrote, "I saw the hideous phantom of a man stretched out, and then, on the working of some powerful engine, show signs of life, and stir with an uneasy, half-vital motion."[1]

Whether born from a flash of inspiration or the product of a time when the wonders of electricity were first being explored, Shelley's *Frankenstein* broke new ground in literature. Featuring the gruesome story of a monster that wreaks havoc on the scientist who created him, *Frankenstein* is one of the earliest examples of a new type of writing called science fiction. Science fiction, or sci-fi, is literature that combines a gripping plot with intriguing speculations about scientific discoveries or future technologies. *Frankenstein* is one of the first sci-fi novels written by a woman.

When *Frankenstein* was published on January 1, 1818, it became an immediate best seller. The novel remains popular to this day. But science fiction didn't really take hold as a genre until the 1900s. And even then,

THE MOTHER OF SCIENCE FICTION

Mary Shelley is often referred to as the mother of science fiction. When she started writing what would become *Frankenstein* in 1816, she was on vacation in Geneva, Switzerland. She was with a group of intellectuals, including her husband, poet Percy Bysshe Shelley, and another poet, Lord Byron. Byron suggested it might be fun for the group to entertain each other by telling ghost stories—and try their hand at writing them. Mary Shelley's story became *Frankenstein*.

To the general public, the actual author of *Frankenstein* was not immediately clear. When it was first published in 1818, it was released anonymously in three volumes, with a preface by Percy Bysshe Shelley. A second edition was published in 1822. The third, published in 1831, is the version that is attributed to Mary.

the idea that women could look beyond the usual female-centric themes like love and family drama to write worthwhile books about ghoulish creatures, space exploration, and more was still too far-fetched for many publishers and readers to accept.

The Dawn of Science Fiction

More than 100 years ago, a number of writers were crafting spellbinding fiction full of new, futuristic themes: aliens, artificial intelligence, and space and time travel. In the late 1800s, books such as British writer H. G. Wells's *The Time Machine*, *The Invisible Man*, and *The War of the Worlds* lined bookstore shelves. New pulp magazines such as Hugo Gernsback's *Amazing Stories* became popular in the 1920s. At the time, science fiction was a male-oriented field—written by men and featuring male protagonists. Though many women read books about technology gone haywire or robots taking over the planet, the notion of female writers actually contributing to the genre was rare.

Toward the mid-1900s, a handful of writers such as Alice B. Sheldon, Catherine Lucille Moore, and Alice Mary Norton circumvented this gender-biased system. They submitted pieces to editors under androgynous or male-sounding pen names—James Tiptree Jr., C. L. Moore, and Andre Norton, respectively—to even the playing field and attract readers. Still, female science fiction writers were far from being recognized on their own terms. It was not until the 1960s and 1970s that women began to break through the gender barrier and publish their own works, using their own names, to a wider audience and on a larger scale.

One of the first women to make waves in the science fiction world was Madeleine L'Engle, although her path to fame was far from smooth. She published five novels under her own name by the time she turned 40 in 1958, but even then L'Engle was not well known by the public. "[W]ith all the hours I spent writing, I was still not pulling my own weight financially," L'Engle later wrote in her memoir *A Circle of Quiet*.[2]

But in 1959, she started working on a new book that features space travel, a disembodied brain, a world under

MALE OR FEMALE?

During the late 1960s, the stories of James Tiptree Jr. started getting attention in the science fiction world. They feature rocket ships, aliens, deadly viruses, and fast-paced narratives that readers loved. The public couldn't get enough of this man's writing!

But in 1976, a secret was uncovered: Tiptree was, in fact, a woman named Alice Sheldon. Sheldon had chosen the pen name to mask her gender in order to get published. The revelation caused much controversy. But it also helped break down the imaginary barrier between "women's writing" and "men's writing."

Today Sheldon's legacy lives on. Every year, a James Tiptree Jr. Literary Award is given to science fiction and fantasy writers of promise who are expanding readers' understanding of gender in literature.

attack by a mysterious force, and a realistic female protagonist—a shocking new development in science fiction. L'Engle hoped she had hit on something big. After two and a half years of writing—and rejections from 26 publishers—*A Wrinkle in Time* was finally published in 1962. The book won the John Newbery Medal as the best children's book of 1963. It has since sold more than 14 million copies.[3]

Not everyone adored L'Engle's *A Wrinkle in Time* when it was released. Some critics thought the book was too religious. Many well-established science fiction writers objected to it because it did not adhere to the genre's traditional setups and resolutions, which feature a lot of action and usually take place on some sort of galactic battlefield. But what makes *A Wrinkle in Time* meaningful and influential—especially to younger readers—is that it is personal. It filters larger themes—good versus evil, conformity versus individuality, and the triumph of love—through the perception of a child. And the author's Newbery win sent a clear message to other women hoping to try their hand at science fiction. If L'Engle could succeed, they could too. One of the first women to heed this call was Ursula K. Le Guin.

Like L'Engle, Le Guin received many rejection letters from agents when she started writing in the 1950s. Though she published four novels and a few stories in the pulp magazines *Fantastic Stories* and *Amazing Stories* in the 1960s, most of her work went unnoticed. This changed when *The Left Hand of Darkness* was released in March 1969. Unlike L'Engle's *A Wrinkle in Time*, Le Guin's novel contains all the common sci-fi elements. It's a story about a human who tries to convince the people of the planet Gethen to join the Ekumen, a League of Worlds. But the politically minded book also features characters that are genderless and ambisexual—a theme largely unexplored in science fiction up until

L'Engle's *A Wrinkle in Time*
was made into a film in 2004.

Le Guin explored themes related to gender in *The Left Hand of Darkness*.

that point. "[The book] was my ignorant approach to feminism," Le Guin said. "I knew just enough to realize that gender itself was coming into question."[4]

The Left Hand of Darkness opened doors for female science fiction authors. Because of Le Guin's avant-garde ideas, other

women writers felt more compelled to expand the genre's boundaries into territory more their own. To this day, authors such as two-time World Fantasy Award–winner Karen Joy Fowler credit Le Guin as the inspiration they needed to write science fiction. "[Le Guin was] extremely influential on me in that area of what I, as a beginning writer, thought a story must look like, and the much more expansive view I have now of what a story can be and can do," Fowler said.[5]

Today's Science Fiction Writers

Thanks to Shelley, L'Engle, Le Guin, and others, science fiction is no longer considered a men-only genre. In the last 50 years, the genre has become a forum for writers to examine social and political issues. Joanna Russ's controversial 1975 novel *The Female Man* includes a planet inhabited entirely by girls and women. The book received both lavish praise and nasty criticism because of its unabashed examination of female sexuality and its underlying message that patriarchal societies limit a woman's rights and opportunities. Author Octavia Butler defied stereotypes by becoming the first female African American to use science fiction to explore matters of race, class, genetics, and prejudice in her works such as the Patternist series, *Kindred*, and the Xenogenesis trilogy.

More recently, a new group of women are being celebrated for advances in science fiction. Award-winning writers such as Kelly Link and Kameron Hurley have burst onto the scene. Newcomer Ann Leckie's 2013 debut novel *Ancillary Justice* won many awards in the genre and—in a nod to Le Guin—features a world full of characters of indistinguishable gender. And Veronica Roth's best-selling Divergent trilogy features a strong female protagonist and is one of the first series to introduce dystopian themes to younger audiences. Today there are more women than ever before producing works in the field. And they're sending a message loud and clear: women in science fiction aren't going away.

FACING OPPOSITION

In 2013, two groups of mostly male science fiction writers and readers—the Sad Puppies and the more conservative Rabid Puppies—complained that fan-nominated and fan-decided science fiction awards like the Hugo were going to too many women and writers of color, whose work they claimed was not up to par. The Puppies also claimed that these writers' works were too political, with plots involving too many social issues.

In 2015, the Puppies learned a lesson when awards season rolled around. They only nominated books by white, straight men, including some books written by authors from the Sad Puppy and Rapid Puppy groups. But when an unprecedented 6,000 fans showed up to vote at Worldcon, none of the Puppies-backed books won. Instead, these Hugo Awards went to writers of color and women.

Veronica Roth enjoys
meeting her fans at
book signings.

Doris Kearns Goodwin made a career for herself writing biographies of US presidents.

CHAPTER FIVE

Nonfiction and Memoir

T hroughout history, most nonfiction was written by men. By the 2010s, more than 80 percent of nonfiction best sellers were the work of male authors. "Nonfiction in particular is a hard nut to crack in terms of gender imbalance," says Erin Belieu, cofounder of VIDA—an organization that examines gender equality issues in contemporary literary culture. "There is a cultural assumption that the hard, factual issues are going to be coming from male writers. This unconscious bias is a self-perpetuating thing that ends up happening."[1]

Despite the gender disparity, a number of female writers in the last 100 years have used the nonfiction form to present deeply influential, impeccably researched ideas about pressing topics. During the 1930s and 1940s, when the words *scientist* and *female* were rarely in the same sentence, marine biologist and activist Rachel Carson wrote trailblazing books about the ecology of oceans. Her 1962 sensation *Silent Spring* advocated for sweeping legislation that would protect the environment for decades to come, earning her the title "mother of the modern environmental movement."[2]

Another field where women were sorely underrepresented was history. According to the American Historical Association, in 1980 women accounted for just 14 percent of the faculty in four-year college and university history departments. In 2007, this number had jumped slightly to less than 35 percent. Yet despite the lack of opportunity, former Harvard University government professor Doris Kearns Goodwin was determined to be the top in her field. She earned a PhD in government from Harvard University in 1968. She served as an assistant to President Lyndon B. Johnson in his last year in the White House and later helped him write his memoirs. From there, she went on to write five award-winning biographies of US presidents and their families, such as the 1995 Pulitzer Prize–winning *No Ordinary Time: Franklin & Eleanor Roosevelt: The Home Front in World War II*.

In addition to looking outward, women of the 1900s and early 2000s also turned a piercing gaze onto themselves by publishing memoirs. This genre of literature has been around for centuries but became especially popular during the 1990s. Memoirs are important because they give readers windows into worlds full of truths and experiences that are not their own. Memoirs by women helped open readers' eyes to the unique challenges women from all walks of life face. Writers published their tell-alls about alcohol abuse, childhood trauma, and sex. In her best-selling 2006 memoir *Eat, Pray, Love,* Elizabeth Gilbert inspired more than ten million women to follow her lead and become world travelers to better understand themselves.

Rachel Carson

Rachel Carson was born on May 27, 1907, in Springdale, Pennsylvania. She started working for the US Bureau of Fisheries in 1936. From there, she rose through the ranks to become editor-in-chief of publications for the US Fish and Wildlife Service, where she stayed until 1952. Over the next 19 years, Carson also published three books: *Under the Sea-Wind*, *The Sea Around Us*, and *The Edge of the Sea*.

But it was Carson's *Silent Spring* that was most influential. The book's criticism of big agriculture and the US government's widespread use of pesticides following World War II triggered the ban of toxic chemicals such as DDT. The book also spurred the formation of the Environmental Protection Agency (EPA) in 1970.

Carson testified before Congress in 1963, advocating for new policies to protect human health, animals, and the environment. Though she died on April 14, 1964, her legacy lives on. "She was the one who kind of rang the alarm bell, that we have to start thinking about the world around us in a different way," said Laurie M. Deredita, curator of a collection of Carson's papers at Connecticut College.[3]

(1907–1964)

Zora Neale Hurston, Jamaica Kincaid, Maxine Hong Kingston, and 2011 National Book Award winner Jesmyn Ward were just some of twentieth-century novelists and poets of color who wrote searing firsthand accounts of influential moments in their lives. *My Brother*, Kincaid's harrowing account of her brother's failed struggle with drugs and AIDS in Antigua, and *Men We Reaped*, Ward's homage to the five African-American loved ones she'd lost to drugs, gang violence, and suicide, helped readers understand the difficulties writers of color were facing. These works facilitated a broader discussion about race, prejudice, and identity in America and around the world.

A Versatile Writer

One of the most gifted nonfiction writers in the last century is journalist Rebecca Solnit. Solnit made a name for herself because of her ability to write about a wide variety of subjects, including climate change, art, and politics. In addition to her journalism in magazines, some of her books include *A Field Guide to Getting Lost*; *As Eve Said to the Serpent: On Landscape, Gender, and Art*; and *The Faraway Nearby*.

Solnit is also well known and admired for another reason. In her essay "Men Explain Things to Me," she coined the term *mansplaining*—when a man

MANSPLAINING MANIFESTO

"Every woman knows what I'm talking about. It's the presumption that makes it hard, at times, for any woman in any field; that keeps women from speaking up and from being heard when they dare; that crushes young women into silence by indicating, the way harassment on the street does, that this is not their world. It trains us in self-doubt and self-limitation just as it exercises men's unsupported overconfidence."[4]

—Rebecca Solnit, "Men Explain Things to Me"

Solnit created the
term *mansplaining*.

lectures a woman about a subject, under the incorrect assumption that she knows less than he does. After Solnit's essay ran in 2008, the article sparked a nationwide feminist call to action. By 2012, the concept of mansplaining had become a fixture in gender-related discussions on blogs and in prominent publications such as the *New York Times* and *Salon*. And in 2014, the word was officially added to the *Oxford Dictionary*.

Immersion Journalism

Another journalist who brought attention to prominent issues is Barbara Ehrenreich. She has written powerful discourses on the origins and history of war, the downside of thinking positively in America, and how science and religion intersect. But Ehrenreich's most groundbreaking nonfiction work was her 2001 book *Nickel and Dimed: On (Not) Getting By in America*.

Ehrenreich went undercover to shed light on the struggles of America's working class. For three months in three different cities during 1998, she disguised herself as an uneducated, unskilled worker. She got jobs in minimum-wage positions as a

MAXINE HONG KINGSTON: WOMAN WARRIOR

In the mid-1970s, two movements were gaining a foothold in America: multiculturalism and feminism. At the intersection was one of the first memoirs to be written by a woman of color about the immigrant experience. *The Woman Warrior: Memoirs of a Girlhood Among Ghosts*, published in 1976, blends myths, family stories, and recollections from the California childhood of its author, second-generation Chinese American Maxine Hong Kingston.

"Coming to a new country isn't easy for anyone. Coming to the United States from China [was] especially hard because the two cultures are so dissimilar," wrote Jonathan Yardley in the *Washington Post*. "*The Woman Warrior* is probably one of the most influential books now in print in this country."[5]

waitress, a maid, a weekend staff member in an Alzheimer's ward, and a cashier at Walmart. Then she wrote a book about how impossible it was to pay rent, afford groceries, and feel confident under such challenging conditions.

Ehrenreich's book was an immediate best seller—and was widely read on many college campuses. More important, it made some Americans think differently about poverty. "We have Barbara Ehrenreich to thank for bringing us the news of America's working poor so clearly and directly, and conveying with it a deep moral outrage and a finely textured sense of lives as lived," wrote one reporter in the *New York Times*.[6]

Wild about Dear Sugar

Like Ehrenreich, Cheryl Strayed has made a significant impact on the minds and hearts of the book-buying public. Inspired by the late Ann Landers and Abigail Van Buren, advice writers of the 1950s, she took over the weekly Dear Sugar column posted on the literary site the *Rumpus* in 2010. She wrote the column anonymously. Before long, Sugar's guidance on romance, breakups, sex, and insecurity became a nationwide phenomenon. At the time, Strayed's work was "some of the most surprising, raw, and heartbreaking writing on the Internet," said reporter Rachel Syme in *Vulture*.[7]

Strayed finally revealed her identity in February 2012. A month later, she published her memoir, *Wild*. The book chronicles her challenging solo journey hiking more than 1,000 miles (1,609 km) of the Pacific Crest Trail from the Mojave Desert through California and Oregon to Washington State. By the end of the year, the book was a *New York Times* best seller, voted the Best Nonfiction Book of

Strayed attended the film premiere for *Wild*, the movie based on her book.

2012 by the *Boston Globe* and *Entertainment Weekly*, and made into a major motion picture. In just two years, Strayed had cemented her place as one of the most beloved writers in America.

Rebecca Solnit, Barbara Ehrenreich, and Cheryl Strayed are just three in a small army of powerhouse female nonfiction writers—and their numbers are growing. Even though women's voices are underrepresented in a genre where men dominate, they have nonetheless had a huge impact on history as they bring women's stories and research to the forefront.

THE ORIGINAL SUGARS

Long before Dear Sugar existed, two identical twins were the pioneers of the modern-day advice column. The twins—Esther Lederer and Pauline Phillips—became celebrated advice columnists who doled out tips and guidance to women, using the pen names Ann Landers and Abigail van Buren.

It all started when Lederer won a contest to replace the original author of the Ask Ann Landers column for the *Chicago Sun-Times* in 1955. Three months later, Phillips started her own column in the *San Francisco Chronicle* called Dear Abby. The dueling columns started a sometimes bitter, sometimes friendly rivalry between the sisters. Before 83-year-old Lederer died in 2002, she was named the most influential woman in the United States by a 1978 World Almanac survey. At the time of 94-year-old Phillips's death in 2013, Dear Abby ran in 1,400 newspapers worldwide, had a readership of more than 110 million, and received more than 10,000 letters and e-mails a week.[8]

Women lead a suffrage
parade in Washington, DC,
on March 3, 1913.

CHAPTER SIX

Feminist Writing

By the year 2000, 60 percent of American women worked. In contrast, only 34 percent of American women held a job in 1950. In those days, most people in society believed that a woman's job was to marry, start a family immediately, and devote her life to homemaking. For many women in the 1950s, this arrangement felt restrictive. But they did not have many other options. Most employers did not consider women for jobs. When they did, it was usually for low-paying positions.

Just a century earlier, women known as suffragists and first-wave feminists fought for women's right to vote. Outspoken leaders such as Susan B. Anthony, Elizabeth Cady Stanton, Lucretia Mott, Carrie Chapman Catt, Alice Paul, and Sojourner Truth held rallies, staged protests, and gave speeches. They demanded equal rights for women. After 70 years of difficult struggle to be recognized, constant mockery by members of the media, and indifference from lawmakers and government officials, their efforts

SIMONE DE BEAUVOIR'S *THE SECOND SEX*

When it was published in France in 1949 and then in the United States in 1953, French existentialist Simone de Beauvoir's *The Second Sex* caused a massive uproar. Some critics thought the 972-page text far too long. The Vatican placed it on the Index of Forbidden Books.

Despite these critiques, *The Second Sex* is widely considered to be one of the catalysts of the second-wave feminist movement. The book condemns the idea that women should be forced to play a secondary role in society to men. "[Simone de Beauvoir] had enormous influence on women of my generation and those which followed," said Beauvoir biographer Huguette Bouchardeau. "She struggled to free herself from conformism and to play the card of freedom."[1]

paid off. On August 18, 1920, the Nineteenth Amendment to the US Constitution was ratified. It granted women the right to vote.

The Nineteenth Amendment was a huge victory for women. It gave them many of the rights already available to men. Women could now own property and have legal right to the money they earned. But by the late 1950s and early 1960s, many women had become frustrated that they still lacked opportunities routinely offered to men. They were called second-wave feminists. Some fought to dismantle workplace inequality. They wanted more freedom when choosing a profession, instead of being limited to traditional women's jobs such as teacher and secretary. They also wanted the ability to advance while earning a livable wage. Others wanted fewer social restrictions. After the birth control pill was made available in 1960, many women wanted more sexual freedom and the right to delay marriage and starting a family. Using the suffragists as their guide and a 1953 feminist book written by the French author Simone de Beauvoir called *The Second Sex*, these women were ready to take action. Words became their most powerful weapon.

Second-Wave Feminists

One writer responsible for igniting the second wave of feminism was Betty Friedan. In *The Feminine Mystique*, Friedan examined what she viewed as an oppressive patriarchal culture in the United States. "Our culture does not permit women to accept or gratify their basic need to grow and fulfill their potentialities as human beings," Friedan wrote in the book.[2]

When it was published in 1963, copies of *The Feminine Mystique* sold rapidly. Friedan, who later helped found the National Organization for Women in 1966 and served as its first president, became famous overnight. The book also served as the inspiration for other feminist writers to lend their voices to the argument for women's rights.

Second-wave feminists, including Betty Friedan, pushed to give women more opportunities outside the home.

The League of
American Pen Women

First lady Eleanor Roosevelt, *center*, was an honored guest at a Pen Women author luncheon in 1933.

In June 1897, writer Marian Longfellow O'Donoghue set out to create a union of female authors in Washington, DC. With fellow journalists Margaret Sullivan Burke and Anna Sanborn Hamilton, the group pulled together other women from poets and novelists to journalists and even educators to form the League of American Pen Women.

The women in the league wanted their work to be taken seriously during a time when too few women were published. The women worked to support each other in their writing careers. They promised they would always be paid for their work as professionals and not give it away for free.

By 1921, the league had expanded with 35 branches across the United States. It also welcomed artists and composers as members. Today, more than 55,000 female writers, artists, and musicians are members of the league.[3] Branches offer workshops, art exhibits, public readings, and other events and programs to promote women in the arts.

A display of books written by Pen Women

In 1970, 34-year-old Kate Millet's *Sexual Politics* was the first academic take on feminist literary criticism—examining the ways in which literature is used to undermine the social, political, and economic oppression of women. It explores the dynamics of power and proves just how often women were being marginalized not just in patriarchal society, but in books and art as well. That same year, the radical Australian-born Germaine Greer's *Female Eunuch* received support for its thesis that the suburban nuclear family repressed women sexually. "[Greer was] living testament to the idea that women don't have to do what has always been expected of them: be good girls, get married, have kids, be nice, and shut up," said *New Statesman* deputy editor Helen Lewis.[4]

THE LAWS BEHIND THE WOMEN'S LIBERATION MOVEMENT

During the 1960s and 1970s, a number of crucial political milestones helped fuel the fire of feminism. In 1960, the Food and Drug Administration approved the birth control pill, giving women the freedom to choose when to have children. In 1972, Congress passed Title IX of the Higher Education Act, which prohibits discrimination on the basis of gender. In 1973, in its controversial ruling on *Roe v. Wade*, the US Supreme Court legalized abortion. And in 1972, Congress passed the Equal Rights Amendment, which prohibits discrimination on the basis of gender and legally claims that men and women are equals. Because it did not receive the 38 "yes" votes from the states, however, the Equal Rights Amendment did not become part of the US Constitution.

But despite Millet and Greer's loud rallying cries, the women's movement was not unified. Many of the speeches and books written during this time addressed problems that white, college-educated, middle-class women faced. Women of color were often left out of the discussion.

To fill the void, civil rights activists Angela Davis and

Florynce Kennedy, and later on second-wave feminist and social activist bell hooks, stepped in. They offered powerful arguments on the evils of racial and class oppression. Kennedy was the only African-American female in her Columbia Law School graduating class in 1951 and a founder of the Feminist Party in 1971. She wrote one of the first books on abortion, called *Abortion Rap*, that same year. Because of her willingness to write about sensitive topics such as rape and abortion, Kennedy gave women of all races a blueprint for a path forward. Justice Emily Jane Goodman of the New York State Supreme Court called her a role model. "She showed a whole generation of us the right way to live our lives," Goodman said.[5]

BELL HOOKS: FEMINIST WARRIOR

Born Gloria Watkins in 1952, bell hooks made a name for herself during the 1980s and 1990s mainly by critiquing feminism. Though a feminist herself, hooks—like other women of color—found fault with the educated, upper-class, mainstream movement for failing to address the day-to-day concerns of nonwhite women.

While she was still an undergraduate at Stanford University, hooks started her first book, *Ain't I a Woman: Black Women and Feminism*. It took more than six years to write, but when it was published in 1981, it was widely praised. Eleven years later, *Publishers Weekly* ranked it among the "twenty most influential women's books of the previous twenty years."[6]

Third-Wave Feminists

In today's third wave of feminism, which began in the 1990s, the attitude toward women's rights has shifted. The idea of feminism has become more widespread. To make room for the change, feminism in the last 20 years has taken on a decidedly different tone. It embraces childless or unmarried women,

Kennedy wrote about subjects that most authors avoided, such as rape and abortion.

working mothers, lesbians, women of color, or any combination of these. The writing has shifted too. Naomi Wolf's 1991 book *The Beauty Myth* argues for a reevaluation of society's standards of beauty. It helped bring about change in the way women are portrayed in the media. Ayelet Waldman was one of the first writers to openly chronicle her boredom with motherhood in *Bad Mother: A Chronicle of Maternal Crimes, Minor Calamities, and Occasional Moments of Grace*, published in 2009. The book brought attention to a new kind of woman—one for whom motherhood isn't always pleasant, comfortable, or even natural. It embraces the variety of experiences women have with motherhood instead of enforcing traditional ideas of women as natural mothers.

But one of the more significant changes in the last three decades is that nonwhite feminists are slowly getting more mainstream attention. One of today's most outspoken feminists is Haitian-American novelist Roxane Gay. *Bad Feminist* is her fierce and often funny *New York Times* best-selling collection of essays. It suggests that one of the feminist movement's biggest failures was not taking women of color, queer women, and transgender women seriously. Gay and other authors like her believe that more can be done to make the voices and experiences of nonwhite women visible.

"I embrace the label of bad feminist because I am human. I am messy. I'm not trying to be an example. I am not trying to be perfect. I am not trying to say I have all the answers. I am not trying to say I'm right. I am just trying—trying to support what I believe in, trying to do some good in this world, trying to make some noise with my writing while also being myself."[7]

—*Roxane Gay,* Bad Feminist

Emily Dickinson did not receive
recognition for her poetry
during her lifetime.

CHAPTER SEVEN

Poetry

Many people are familiar with the names Emily Dickinson, Elizabeth Barrett Browning, and Christina Rossetti. These poets lived and wrote during the 1800s. They set a powerful precedent when they were recognized for their craft during a time when most published poetry was written by men. Dickinson is considered one of the greatest American poets, male or female. She also took on some women's issues in her writing. In some of her poems, she wrote about the lack of freedom and choice that married women suffered during her time.

At the time these women were writing, published female poets were rare. Even by 1900, successful female poets were uncommon. But over the next hundred years, the gender disparity in poetry slowly began to change. By the end of the 1900s and into the 2000s, the prospect that a woman could be respected as a poet was an attainable—and frequent—reality.

While much of the enthusiasm surrounding poetry in the early 1900s still focused on male writers such as T. S. Eliot and Robert Frost, a few women managed to break through the barricades. Though not well known

EMILY DICKINSON

Emily Dickinson was born on December 10, 1830, in Amherst, Massachusetts. She attended Mount Holyoke Female Seminary in 1847 but left after one year. For most of her life, Dickinson preferred to stay indoors. She isolated herself from the public, staying close to her family.

Books and poetry were Dickinson's salvation. She read countless volumes of Robert and Elizabeth Barrett Browning's work, as well as poems by John Keats. When she died in 1886, Dickinson was still unknown as an accomplished poet. But after her death, her family discovered 40 hand-bound volumes of nearly 1,800 poems.[2] When these were published over a 65-year period from 1890 to 1955, Dickinson earned her reputation as one of the greatest poets in American history.

now, Sara Teasdale was the first person—male or female—to win the Pulitzer in poetry, then called the Columbia University Poetry Society Prize. She won in 1918 for her collection *Love Songs*. This lyrical and sweeping collection explores love, death, and beauty from a woman's perspective.

A contemporary of Teasdale, Edna St. Vincent Millay was a poet of a different sort. Openly bisexual during an era when such behavior was frowned upon, she published a volume of poetry called *A Few Figs from Thistles* in 1920. The collection shocked critics because of its detailed descriptions of female sexuality. "Rarely [had a woman] written as outspokenly as Millay," wrote critic Carl Van Doren.[1] But that did not stop Millay from becoming the fifth person—and third woman—to win the Pulitzer Prize in 1923. Her work would serve as an inspiration for generations of poets who wished to write about less conventional ideas of love, sex, romance, and marriage.

Confessional Poets

By the late 1950s, the world—and a woman's role in it—had begun changing. So had the poetry. Male poets such as Jack Kerouac and Allen Ginsberg still claimed the voice of the 1950s Beat Generation. These writers and artists lived on the fringes of society and frequently wrote about the benefits of drug use and freer ways of thinking. But the confessional period of the 1960s was a different story. Confessional poets Anne Sexton and Sylvia Plath were outspoken about their feelings. They wrote intimately about subject matters that had previously been off-limits—death, anxiety, depression, and troubled relationships. And they did so by disclosing details about their personal lives.

Though her fans adored her, critics chided Anne Sexton for writing honestly about menstruation, abortion, and the years she spent suffering from the psychiatric illness that would eventually kill her. "At the [time] everyone said, 'You can't write this way. It's too personal; it's confessional; you can't write this, Anne,'"[3] she recalled in an interview. But Sexton would not be silenced. She wrote more than ten books of poems. In 1967, she won a Pulitzer Prize for *Live or Die*, her third collection about recovering from a mental breakdown.

Like Sexton, author Sylvia Plath faced mental health challenges. Plath produced a semiautobiographical novel called *The Bell Jar* and a number of poetry collections, including *Ariel* and the Pulitzer Prize–winning *Selected Poems*. Plath committed suicide in 1963 at the age of 31. But her works turned her into one of the most respected female American poets of the 1900s by both readers and poetry scholars.

Sexton holds a copy of her award-winning
book, *Live or Die*.

Black Arts Innovators

Around the same time Sexton and Plath were writing, an exciting new movement called the Black Arts movement was taking shape in the poetry world during the 1960s and 1970s. It found its roots in the Harlem Renaissance, an era during the 1920s and 1930s when music, visual art, and poetry by African Americans thrived in New York and spread throughout the world. Bolstered by the political work being done by pro–black power groups such as the Black Panthers, the Black Arts movement was motivated by African-American artists' desire to create politically engaged poetry that explored their cultural experience. Gwendolyn Brooks and Nikki Giovanni were instrumental in the scene.

An early member of the movement, Gwendolyn Brooks was a poet of firsts. She was the first African-American woman to win the Pulitzer Prize for Poetry in 1950 for *Annie Allen*. This collection of poems examined the urban poor and the role of women in society. In 1968, Brooks was appointed to the prestigious position of poet laureate of Illinois. She became the first African-American poetry consultant to the Library of Congress in 1985 at the age of 68.

SYLVIA PLATH'S *BELL JAR*

Critics praised Sylvia Plath's only novel, *The Bell Jar*, for being a triumphantly feminist yet terrifying record of a woman's suffering. "Perhaps being born a woman is part of the exceptional rasp of her nature, a woman whose stack of duties was laid over the ground of genius, ambition, and grave mental instability," *New York Review* book critic Elizabeth Hardwick wrote in 1971.[4]

Plath may have been unsure about what the book's reception would be when it was published in 1963. In fact, she initially did so using the pseudonym Victoria Lucas. But she needn't have worried. *The Bell Jar* became a milestone for generations of readers hoping for an insight into mental illness and the ill effects of a repressive 1950s society on women.

The Black Arts *Movement*

Toni Morrison was a major player in the Black Arts movement.

In the decade between 1965 and 1975, a new artistic movement was sweeping the country. Inspired by the civil rights and Black Power movements, a wave of African-American artists took the teachings of Dr. Martin Luther King and Malcolm X and used them to create courageous works of art in a wide range of mediums.

The Black Arts Repertory Theatre was founded in Harlem, New York, in 1965. And jazz musicians such as Thelonious Monk and John Coltrane flourished as their music became the soundtrack for African-American writers everywhere, including Maya Angelou, Sonia Sanchez, Toni Morrison, and Audre Lorde.

The Black Arts movement began in New York and spread to Chicago, Illinois; San Francisco; and Detroit, Michigan. Though it faded out in 1975, the art helped lay the foundation for more modern art forms such as hip-hop, rap, and spoken word poetry.

The civil rights and Black Power movements
sparked the Black Arts movement.

Brooks made a big impact on the world of poetry.

Brooks had "a unique position in American letters," said Afro-American literature professor George E. Kent. "Not only [had] she combined a strong commitment to racial identity and equality with a mastery of poetic techniques, but she [also] managed to bridge the gap between the academic poets of her generation in the 1940s and the young black militant writers of the 1960s."[5]

Nikki Giovanni was another Black Arts member, but a more radical one. In 1968, she self-published her first collection of poems, *Black Feeling Black Talk*. The collection was a righteous call for black unity and revolutionary action against a racist white system. In its first year, the book sold more than 10,000 copies.[6] Later that same year, she released a follow-up volume of poetry covering the same issues called *Black Judgment*, which also did well.

Giovanni's fame, not just among African Americans but people of all races, kept growing. She was called "the Princess of Black Poetry" by the *New York Times* and in 1970 was named "Woman of the Year" by *Ebony* magazine.[7] She was also a key founder of the spoken word movement in the late 1980s and early 1990s. This new type of poetry enabled writers to craft bold, often political, poetry about prominent issues such as sexism, racial discrimination, or rape and perform it in front of a live audience. Spoken word became so popular in artistic circles that it inspired new forms of music such as hip-hop and rap: rhythm and poetry put to music.

Contemporary Poets

In the last quarter of the 1900s and into the present, poetry has continued to evolve and reflect the changing attitudes toward our increasingly multicultural world. During the 1980s and 1990s, women such as Palestinian-American Naomi Shihab Nye and Mexican-American Sandra Cisneros found hard-won recognition by living unconventional lives and writing unconventional poetry. Born to a Palestinian father and an American mother and having spent her

"When you're an immigrant writer, or an immigrant, you're not always welcome to this country unless you're the right immigrant. If you have a Mexican accent, people look at you like, you know, 'where do you come from and why don't you go back to where you came from?' . . . . I didn't marry. I didn't have children. I followed the food supply for jobs. I kept writing at night. And that kept me moving. It kept my life disruptive. It broke up many relationships. Was it worth it? Yes."[8]

—*Sandra Cisneros*

childhood in Missouri, Texas, and Jerusalem, Nye brought a global perspective to her poetry. She allowed readers to experience the world not just from an American's point of view but through the eyes of a woman who spent her life traveling throughout Asia, Europe, Mexico, and the Middle East.

In 1984, Cisneros published her groundbreaking novel-in-verse *The House on Mango Street* about a working-class Mexican-American immigrant family in Chicago. She gave voice to Latinos, a group often ignored in the American arts scene.

Today, innovative forms of poetry are as popular as ever. Inspired by the spoken word albums of poet legends such as Maya Angelou and Nikki Giovanni, poetry slam—an event where poets compete and perform their own poetry—is once again on the rise. And in 2014, the first all-women, all-minority team in New York City's poetry slam history competed at the twenty-fifth annual National Poetry Slam.

But why did it take so long, asked Mahogany L. Browne, curator of the Nuyorican Poets Café's poetry program in New York. "The fact that there has never been an all-woman team from the New York or New Jersey area in the last thirty years of slam is an interesting analysis of the community which chooses the slammer to represent the area, as well as the voices that touch the stage," said Browne. "I think when you have a marginalized voice collaborate creatively, it is a powerful thing."[9]

Cisneros speaks at the 2014 Los Angeles
Times Festival of Books.

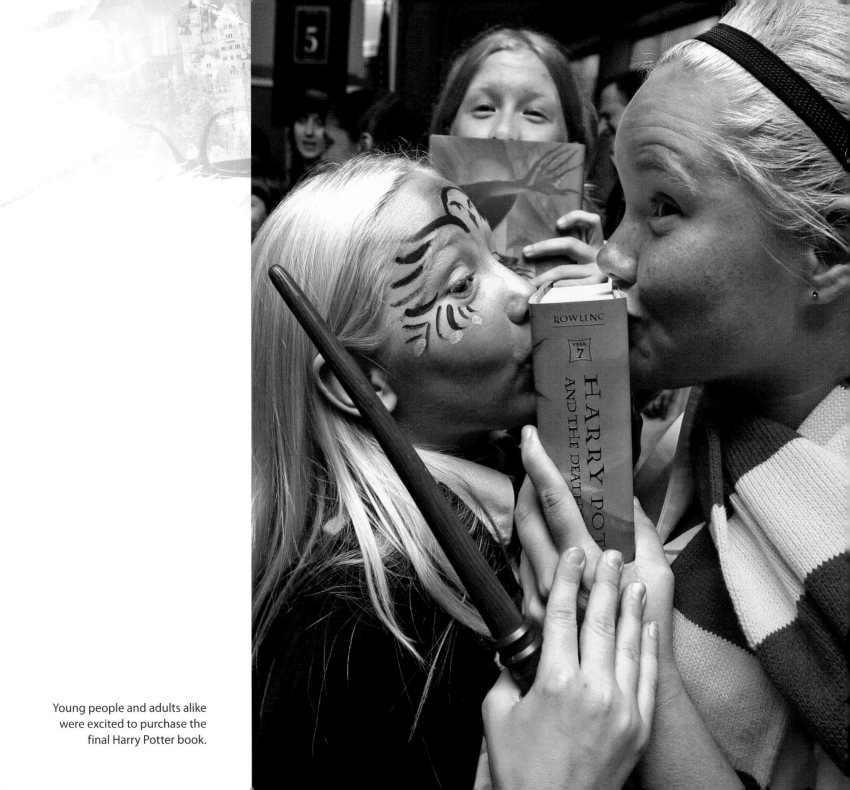

Young people and adults alike were excited to purchase the final Harry Potter book.

CHAPTER EIGHT

Young Adult Literature

In the early 2000s, J. K. Rowling's influential Harry Potter series launched a craze of adults reading children's books. Stephenie Meyer's vampire-themed Twilight quartet triggered a nationwide obsession with vampires. With the first book published in 2008, Suzanne Collins's Hunger Games trilogy spawned a thrilling new era of dystopian fiction. These blockbuster books written for young adults in the early 2000s have transformed the reading experience for people young and old.

Today, young Americans under age 30 are more likely than those 30 and older to report reading a book at least weekly.[1] Still, 55 percent of young adult, or YA, novels are actually purchased by adults. Twenty-eight percent of these adults are between 33 and 44 years old.[2] With an average of 30,000 YA books published annually and sales close to $2.87 billion every year, it's clear these books are popular.[3]

But books written specifically for teens were not always available. Today, the term *young adult* is used to refer to people between the ages of 12 and 18. But it's a fairly new term. *Young adult* was first used in the 1960s by the Young Adult Library Services Association. The evolution of young adult literature into the multibillion-dollar industry it is today took time—and it all started because of a teenage woman.

A NEW DEMOGRAPHIC: TEENAGERS

When looking at a snapshot of the 1800s, historians divide people into two basic groups: adults and children. But beginning in the 1920s, there was a shift. Parents started keeping their kids out of work and in school for longer. People got married later than before—instead of 16 or 17, young people waited until they were in their 20s. Retailers also began to recognize high school students, especially girls, as consumers with specific preferences in clothes and music. By the 1940s, a new demographic was clearly visible: the teenager.

The Birth of a New Genre

Young adult literature has its roots in the years during World War II (1939–1945). Before that time, books such as Louisa May Alcott's *Little Women*, Lucy Maud Montgomery's *Anne of Green Gables*, and Laura Ingalls Wilder's *Little House on the Prairie* were mostly geared either toward young children or adults. Then, in 1942, the situation shifted. A book called *Seventeenth Summer* by college student Maureen Daly was published. The then-progressive novel tells the story of a first crush between an 18-year-old high school basketball star from Oklahoma and a 17-year girl from Chicago. It was the perfect story for the newly established "teenage" audience. "For [1942], this [protagonist] is a pretty avant-garde young woman: she smokes, she drinks, she dates. She thinks about more than a chaste kiss at the end of a date," Teri Lesesne, a professor of library science at Sam Houston State University, told the *New York Times*.[4]

It would take 20 more years for the trend to firmly take root. But by the 1960s and 1970s, writers—most of them women—were eager to follow in Daly's footsteps. S. E. Hinton's trendsetting 1967 debut *The Outsiders* was written when the author was just 17 years old. Featuring a gritty story about feuding teenagers on the fringes of society, the novel is one of the best-selling young adult books of all time.

Some experts argue that the young adult genre would not have gotten off the ground if it had not been for Judy Blume. Her 1970 novel *Are You There God? It's Me, Margaret* broke many barriers in the young adult market. The book talks openly about formerly taboo subjects such as menstruation and puberty. The praise for Blume's writing was positive. She kept on addressing controversial subjects in later books—beauty and body image in *Deenie*, bullying and being overweight in *Blubber*, and responsible teenage sex in *Forever*.

These discussions of controversial topics served as helpful reminders for young readers. Her words were relatable and something to learn from.

"There was only a handful of books having teenage protagonists: Mary Jane wants to go to the prom with the football hero and ends up with the boy next door and has a good time anyway. That didn't ring true to my life. I was surrounded by teens and I couldn't see anything going on in those books that had anything to do with real life."[5]

—S. E. Hinton, author of The Outsiders

YA Books
By the Numbers

A 2015 study by the publishing company Blooming Twig examined 50 books from *Time* magazine's Best Young Adult Books list and the Newbery Award and Honor List published over 200 years. The goal was to see how the popularity of YA books had changed over time. The increase in the popularity of YA can be seen in the first graph.

BOOKS ON *TIME'S* BEST YA BOOKS LIST BY YEAR

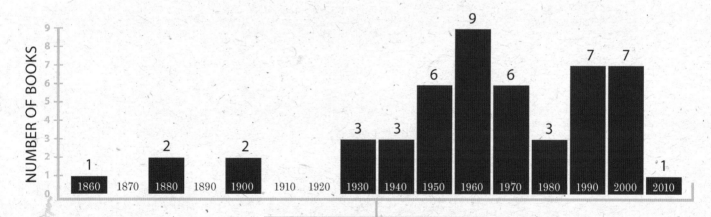

The study also looked at gender bias. Most of the books selected focused on male protagonists and were written by male authors. Additionally, it was most common for male authors to write about male protagonists and for female authors to write about female protagonists.

GENDER IN *TIME*'S BEST YA BOOKS LIST

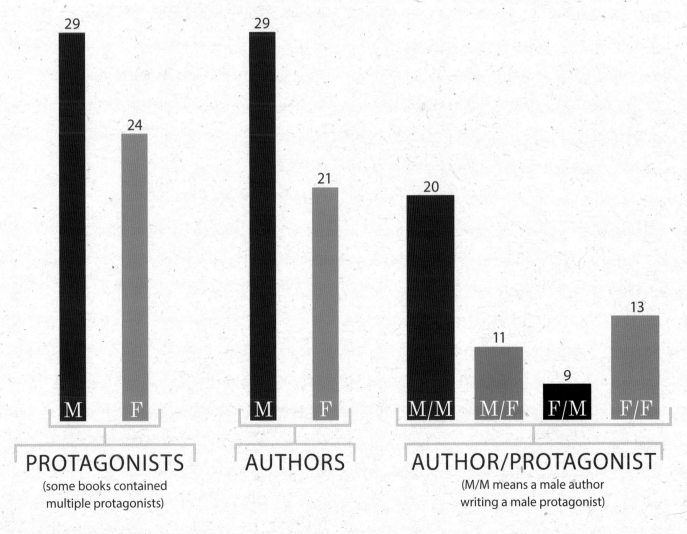

PROTAGONISTS
(some books contained
multiple protagonists)

AUTHORS

AUTHOR/PROTAGONIST
(M/M means a male author
writing a male protagonist)

New York Times journalist Susan Dominus said in 2015,

> For those of us who were teenagers in the early [1980s] and in the decade before . . . there was no Internet; there was just Judy Blume, planting the radical idea, for generations of women, that their bodies would be, should be, a source of pleasure and not of shame. Her credibility was total, a young person's raw perspective, filtered—subtly—through the common sense of a frank, funny woman.[6]

The Second Golden Age of YA

In the two decades following Hinton and Blume's first novels, most of the YA books published—such as Francine Pascal's Sweet Valley High and V. C. Andrews's Flowers in the Attic series—were for middle-grade readers and preteens. Some were even churned out in mass quantities by ghostwriters, people hired to write material for authors using the authors' names. But at the turn of the millennium and continuing on through the next 15 years, the public's appetite for books containing teen-centric themes such as love, sexual experimentation, and even drugs and death exploded. And once again, many women authors were eager to make a name for themselves in the genre.

In the 1990s and 2000s, female YA authors working across all genres—literary fiction, science fiction and fantasy, and nonfiction—wrote books for young readers and started new trends in publishing. Veronica Roth and Cassandra Clare took the sci-fi/fantasy world by storm with their respective Divergent and Mortal Instruments series. Maureen Johnson, Sarah Dessen, and Gayle Forman captured the teen love-and-angst market with books such as *13 Little Blue Envelopes*, *The Truth about Forever*, and *If I Stay*, respectively. And Patricia McCormick, Jenny Downham, and Ellen

Judy Blume is famous for
writing about topics that
teenage girls can relate to.

YA novels are sometimes made into feature films that draw thousands to the theater.

Hopkins wrote about little-explored topics in teen literature, including child trafficking, terminal cancer, and drugs.

"It's not surprising that YA is always dealing with transformation, whether it be realistic or supernatural," said author and publisher Lizzie Skurnick. "It's the only genre that can always be both. It shows teen life in full chaos. And that means constant change."[7]

We Need Diverse Books Movement

But though many women were experiencing great success in young adult publishing, other authors were proportionally absent from classroom libraries and bookstore shelves. They were female writers of color. Then, on April 17, 2014, a Twitter exchange took place between Korean-American YA fantasy author Ellen Oh and Chinese-American YA fantasy author Malinda Lo. They were frustrated by the usually all-white, all-male panels at popular publishing conventions. As one study reported, of the 3,200 children's books published in 2013, there were only 93 about African Americans, 34 about Native Americans, 69 about Asian Americans, and 57 about Latin Americans.[8] Many authors and readers alike wanted to see more diversity in new literature.

By April 29, publishers and members of the media alike had taken notice of the tweets. The #WeNeedDiverseBooks movement was born. It spurred a new focus on multicultural books by authors about topics such as the immigrant experience and teenage pregnancy. Pivotal award-winning novels were brought back into the public eye, including African-American Angela Johnson's *The First Part Last*, Japanese-American Cynthia Kadohata's *Kira-Kira*, and *The Lightning Dreamer*, by Margarita Engle, a Cuban American. Publishers promised to not only put out more works by established writers of color but also to seek new nonwhite talent. And articles by prominent news outlets and social media campaigns helped ensure the cause was front and center.

Slowly, the attitude toward publishing diverse books is changing. In 2014, African-American and young people's poet laureate Jacqueline Woodson won the National Book

THE DIVERSITY GAP IN CHILDREN'S BOOKS

In February 2015, the Cooperative Children's Book Center (CCBC) released the results of a study on the number of children's books by and about people of color published in 2014. The statistics showed that, of the more than 3,000 books the CCBC reviews each year, the amount of books written by and about people of color was 14 percent.[9]

Johnson is the author of the award-winning
YA novel *The First Part Last*.

Award for Young People's Literature, a Newbery Honor, a Coretta Scott King Author Award,

and an NAACP Image Award for Outstanding Work for Teens for her luminous coming-of-age

memoir-in-verse *Brown Girl Dreaming*. In addition to receiving these honors, Woodson has long

been recognized as a role model for future writers because of her tireless efforts to, in her own

words, "write stories that have been historically absent in this country's body of literature"[10]

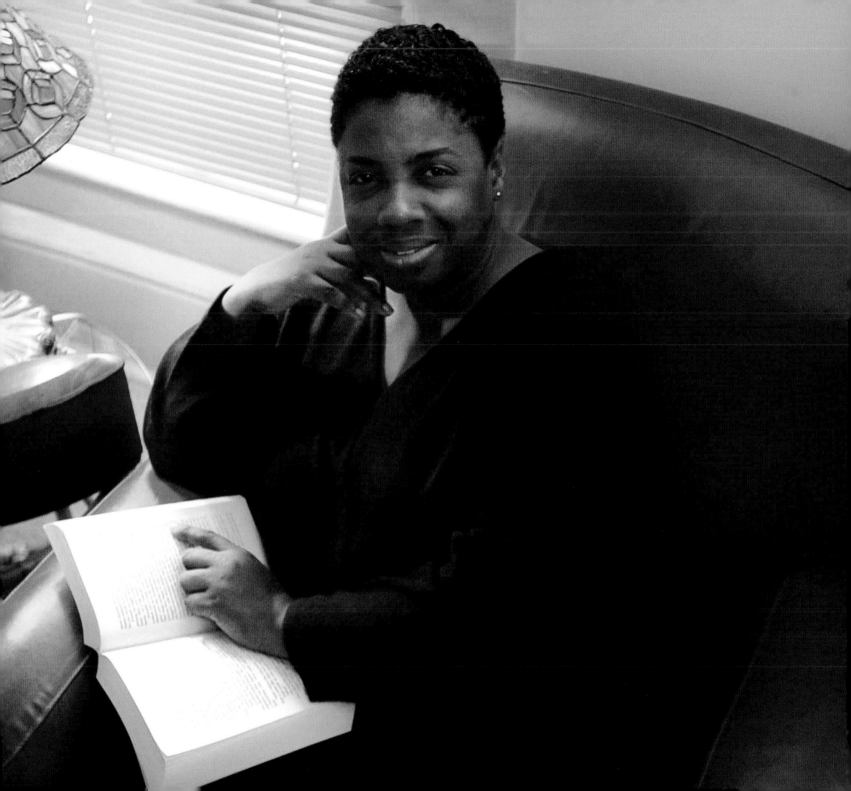

Roxane Gay accepted the 2015
PEN Center USA Freedom to
Write Award.

CHAPTER NINE

Today's Literary Stars

I n February 2011, VIDA—a women-in-publishing advocacy group— released the results of what had become an industry-changing annual study since it started in 2009. The study surveyed 14 American and British literary publications, such as the *New York Times Book Review* and the *Paris Review*, to determine the percentage of female contributors, female book reviewers, and reviews of books by women.

Research showed that most books reviewed by those publications were written by men. An even higher percentage of book critics hired to write the reviews were also men. In a separate study, VIDA surveyed the catalogs of all the major and smaller publishing houses. They found that women writers accounted for approximately 30 percent of the list. Small independent presses were the most male-heavy.

The following year, writer and professor Roxane Gay conducted her own study—this time about race. With the help of a graduate student, she gathered every book review that ran in the *New York Times* in 2011. Then she identified the race and gender of each reviewed title's author. Out of 742 books reviewed across all genres, 655 were written by Caucasian authors. Thirty-one were written by Africans or African Americans; 9 by Hispanic authors; 33 by Asian, Asian-American, or South Asian writers; 8 by Middle Eastern writers; and 6 were books written by writers whose racial background could not be identified in Gay's research.[1]

Nearly 90 percent of books the *New York Times* chose to review in 2011 were written by white people. A majority—437 books—were written by white men. Gay reflected on the results of the study:

> If you are a writer of color, not only do you face a steeper climb getting your book published, you face an even more arduous journey if you want that book to receive critical attention. It shouldn't be this way. Writers deserve that same fighting chance regardless of who they are.[2]

New Horizons in Comics

Judging by the results of VIDA's research and Gay's study, there is mounting evidence that white men are getting most of the attention in the publishing industry. In both the quantity of books published and the media attention their books are receiving, women and multicultural authors are lagging far behind. Still, female writers have begun infiltrating a number of traditionally male-dominated fields, one of which is comics.

Back in 1938 when a bespectacled man named Clark Kent first transformed into Superman, female representation in comics was virtually nonexistent. Jackie Ormes—the first African-American cartoonist—made a splash in 1937 with her *Torchy Brown* and *Patty-Jo 'n' Ginger* comic strips. Contrary to typical images or stories at the time, which usually depicted African Americans as servants or slaves, Ormes's African-American heroines were role models. Ormes's Torchy was classy and clever while Ginger was attractive, assertive, and college-educated. Her comic strips openly discussed pressing social issues such as racism, political campaigns, and controversial events in the news. "[She] was giving voice to what was in the hearts and minds of so many people: [the desire] to move forward and make progress," said Nancy Goldstein, an Ormes biographer.[3]

Later, in 1978, cartoonist Roz Chast followed Ormes's lead when she started creating cartoons for the *New Yorker*, a magazine run mostly by older men at that time. The process was intimidating. But she persisted and soon developed quite a

Ormes wrote comics that feature African-American characters.

following because of her humorous but poignant depictions of Americans' anxieties and neuroses. After her graphic memoir about taking care of her aging parents, *Can't We Talk about Something More Pleasant?*, was published to great acclaim in 2014, Chast solidified her reputation as one of America's most accomplished graphic artists. Yet despite Ormes and Chast's success, for many years women in comics were few and far between.

But the outlook for women in comics is slowly changing. Publishers including DC Comics are acquiring more graphic novels and comics created by women who explore personal topics such as relationships, inequality in the workplace, and whether to have children. "I can still see things moving forward," says *Gotham Academy* comics creator Becky Cloonan. "Being more inclusive allows for more diverse stories to be told, which in turn allows for a larger readership, which feeds back into allowing for more creators."[4]

ROZ CHAST: COMICS PIONEER

Legendary comics pioneer Roz Chast started creating comics for the *New Yorker* in 1978. Since then, she has illustrated nearly 800 more. In 2014, she published a graphic memoir about her aging parents' final years entitled *Can't We Talk about Something More Pleasant?*, which received the first Kirkus Prize and the National Book Critics Circle Award for autobiography. It was also the first graphic novel to be named a finalist for the nonfiction National Book Award. In 2015, she won the Heinz Award. The prize came with $250,000 in cash.

The Internet has also made it possible for fledgling female comics to post and promote their work online, therefore attracting a broader audience. One of the biggest names in comics is *New York Times* best selling artist Canadian Kate Beaton. Her webcomic *Hark! A Vagrant* is a

Becky Cloonan received an Eisner
Award at the 2013 Comic-Con
International Convention.

humorous feminist reexamination of history and literature. It attracts the attention of millions of fans worldwide. The collection—released in book form in 2011—made *Time*'s Best of the Year list. In 2015, Beaton released a second collection entitled *Step Aside, Pops*, which includes more amusing comics of historical events shown from a woman's perspective. Beaton reflected on her work, "I think that honestly [my work] is a response to the larger conversation that we're all having about women's roles in pop culture and media, and in the workforce and in life."[5]

THE PRINCESS AND THE PONY

Comics artist Kate Beaton has a massive online following, thanks to her webcomic *Hark! A Vagrant*. In 2015, she became a children's book author too. Her first picture book, called *The Princess and the Pony*, is about a little princess who doesn't quite get the horse that she wanted for her birthday. What she *does* get is a bit smaller—and dumpier.

"It's a story about love in the end, because her parents love her, they want to support her," Beaton said about the book. "[Princess Pinecone] understands that it's not exactly what she asked for, but she makes the best of it. And then it turns out to be the best gift of all, which also happens, because you treasure those things, because of the love that was behind them."[6]

LGBTQ Advances

Another area where women writers have seen significant advances is in the area of LGBTQ-related publishing. Books written about homosexuals or gender fluidity have become more widespread in recent years. In 2004, *Luna*, a novel about a transgender teen's struggle for self-identity and acceptance, was published, and the world took notice. Transgender author

Julie Anne Peters's *Luna* became a finalist for the National Book Award in Young People's Literature in 2004. It was the first young adult book featuring a transgender protagonist that was released by a major publisher to pick up this honor. Since then, more and more publishers have followed suit. David Levithan, vice president and publisher of Scholastic Press, remarked, "As our culture is starting to acknowledge transgender people and acknowledge that they are part of the fabric of who we are, literature is reflecting that."[7]

Perhaps one of the best examples of women who have built on the accomplishments of their forerunners to make great strides in LGBTQ-themed publishing is Alison Bechdel. Outspoken about her experiences as a lesbian and the daughter of a closeted gay father, Bechdel has many fans. Her *Dykes to Watch Out For* was one of the first comic strips to boldly and humorously describe the trials of being a lesbian in the United States. Her graphic memoir *Fun Home: A Family Tragicomic*, the story of her coming out and her relationship with her father, and *Are You My Mother?: A Comic Drama*, a

THE BECHDEL TEST

The Bechdel Test is a way to measure gender bias in movies. Alison Bechdel made reference to it in her comic strip *Dykes to Watch Out For*. Since then, the test has been used by millions to determine whether women are getting enough representation in cinema. The test involves the following three questions:

- Does the movie have at least two main female characters (who are named)?
- Do the female characters talk to each other?
- Do they talk about something other than a man?

If the answer is yes to all three of those questions, the movie passes the Bechdel test.

follow-up about her strained relationship with her mother, were released in 2006 and 2012 respectively. Bechdel was awarded a MacArthur "Genius" grant in 2014.

What the Future Will Bring

From groundbreaking graphic novels and memoirs to soulful poetry and authoritative nonfiction, women writers continue to forge new paths in publishing. The YA market expands while more and more women are winning prizes in poetry and science fiction. Thanks to the rapid growth of online publishing, the work produced by women in blogs and ebooks is finding new audiences.

Nonetheless, books written by women and women of color are still in the minority. The #WeNeedDiverseBooks campaign is a step to ensuring more multicultural books reach children and adults of all ages and races. The VIDA count has already prompted publishers and media publications to publish and review more books written by women. As Roxane Gay wrote in the *Rumpus* in 2013, "the numbers do mean something. They do matter. At some point, we have to move beyond historical inequities as an explanation."[8] But the fight for equal representation in literature is far from over. There is still work to be done.

Timeline

1818

Mary Shelley's *Frankenstein* is published. It is considered to be the first female-written science fiction novel.

1878

The Leavenworth Case, the first female-written detective novel, is published by Anna Katherine Green.

1918

Sara Teasdale becomes the first person to win the Pulitzer Prize for Poetry.

1942

The first YA book, Maureen Daly's *Seventeenth Summer*, is published.

1950

Gwendolyn Brooks becomes the first African-American woman to win the Pulitzer Prize for Poetry for her collection *Annie Allen*.

1953

Simone de Beauvoir's *The Second Sex* is published in the United States.

1962

Rachel Carson's groundbreaking *Silent Spring* is published, spurring the formation of the Environmental Protection Agency.

1963

Betty Friedan publishes *The Feminine Mystique*, sparking the second wave of feminism.

1965

The Black Arts movement begins in the United States.

1970

Judy Blume's groundbreaking YA novel *Are You There God? It's Me, Margaret* is published.

1982

Alice Walker's novel *The Color Purple* is published. It wins the National Book Award and the first Pulitzer in literature for an African-American woman.

1993

Toni Morrison becomes the first African-American woman to win the Nobel Prize in Literature.

2004

Julie Anne Peters's *Luna* is published, a milestone for LGBTQ-themed books and LGBTQ writers.

2009

VIDA, the advocacy group for women in literature, is formed.

2014

The #WeNeedDiverseBooks campaign begins.

2014

The first all-women, all-minority team in New York City's poetry slam history competes at the twenty-fifth annual National Poetry Slam.

Essential Facts

KEY PLAYERS

- Maya Angelou, a civil rights activist, member of the Black Arts movement, memoirist, playwright, poet, and singer

- Alison Bechdel, a cartoonist and graphic novelist best known for her comic strip *Dykes to Watch Out For* and her recent graphic memoirs *Fun Home: A Family Tragicomic* and *Are You My Mother?: A Comic Drama*

- Barbara Ehrenreich, a nonfiction author and political journalist who was one of the first female writers to pioneer undercover journalism in her book *Nickel and Dimed: On (Not) Getting By in America*

- Ursula K. Le Guin, a pioneer in crafting science fiction when female writers were few and far between

- Jacqueline Woodson, an outspoken advocate for both civil and gender rights who writes about characters from a variety of races, ethnicities, and social classes and is the author of the National Book Award–winning novel-in-verse *Brown Girl Dreaming*

WOMEN AS AUTHORS

Female authors have had to work hard to break into various fields and genres of literature that have been traditionally male-dominated. It was first considered acceptable for women to write only about domestic topics or light romances. But as more women pushed the boundaries, slowly more opportunities opened up to them. Women's writing is still published and reviewed less than writing by men.

IMPACT ON SOCIETY

Throughout the twentieth century, women fought for their basic rights during times when they were seen as less than men. Yet in the face of this overarching struggle, female writers of all races and colors were key in changing things. In their feminist essays, they argued for equal opportunity in the workplace and the right to be seen as something other than wives and mothers. In their works of nonfiction, they not only became authorities on pressing political and economic matters but also influenced social norms and trends. And in their literary fiction, romance novels, and poetry, they crafted award-winning stories both as a means of self-expression and as a way for their readers to connect to and understand the world.

QUOTE

"One isn't necessarily born with courage, but one is born with potential. Without courage, we cannot practice any other virtue with consistency. We can't be kind, true, merciful, generous, or honest."

—*Maya Angelou*

Glossary

ANDROGYNOUS
Of indeterminate sex.

ANONYMOUS
Not named or identified.

AVANT-GARDE
New or experimental ideas, especially in the arts.

BISEXUAL
A person who is physically, romantically, or sexually attracted to members of both sexes.

CHASTE
Morally pure; not having sex.

CIVIL RIGHTS
Enforceable privileges of citizens to personal and political liberties such as freedom of speech, the right to vote, and social equality.

DISEMBODIED
Separated from or existing without the body.

DISPARITY
A great difference.

DYSTOPIAN
A type of utterly horrible or degraded society that is generally headed to an irreversible oblivion.

FEMINISM
The belief that women should have the same opportunities and rights as men politically, socially, and economically.

GENRE
A specific type of music, film, or writing.

LGBTQ
An acronym used to describe nonheterosexual people: lesbian, gay, bisexual, transgender, and queer or questioning.

NOIR
Crime fiction featuring hard-boiled cynical characters and bleak, gritty settings.

PATRIARCHAL
Characteristic of a system of society or government controlled by men.

POET LAUREATE
A celebrated poet officially appointed by a government or institution, who is often expected to compose poems for special events and occasions.

PRECEDENT
An earlier event or action that is regarded as an example to be considered in later similar circumstances.

PREFACE
An introduction to a book, typically stating its subject, scope, or aims.

PROTAGONIST
A main character in a text or play.

PSEUDONYM
A fictitious name, especially one used by an author.

STEREOTYPE
A widely held but oversimplified idea about a particular type of person or thing.

TRANSGENDER
Identifying with a gender other than the one recognized and assigned at birth.

Additional Resources

SELECTED BIBLIOGRAPHY

Kenschaft, Lori, Roger Clark, and Desiree Ciambrone. *Gender Inequality in Our Changing World: A Comparative Approach*. London: Routledge, 2015. Print.

"Official Campaign Site." *WeNeedDiverseBooks.org*. We Need Diverse Books, n.d. Web. 2 Nov. 2015.

Strickland, Ashley. "A Brief History of Young Adult Literature." *CNN.com*. Turner Broadcasting System, Inc., 15 Apr. 2015. Web. 2 Nov. 2015.

"The 2014 VIDA Count." *VIDAweb.org*. VIDA: Women in Literary Arts, n.d. Web. 2 Nov. 2015.

FURTHER READINGS

Anderson, Jennifer Joline. *Women's Rights Movement*. Minneapolis, MN: Abdo, 2014. Print.

Gilbert, Sandra M., and Susan Gubar, eds. *The Norton Anthology of Literature by Women*. New York: Norton, 2007. Print.

Lusted, Marcia Amidon. *The Fight for Women's Suffrage*. Minneapolis, MN: Abdo, 2012. Print.

WEBSITES

To learn more about Women's Lives in Literature, visit **booklinks.abdopublishing.com**. These links are routinely monitored and updated to provide the most current information available.

FOR MORE INFORMATION

For more information on this subject, contact or visit the following organizations:

The American Writers Museum
180 N. Michigan Avenue
Chicago, IL 60601
312-346-9018
http://americanwritersmuseum.org
Set to open in 2017, the American Writers Museum will showcase a rotating set of themed galleries, interactive displays, and educational programs for visitors about the personal lives, homes, and literary accomplishments of American authors.

The Library of Congress
101 Independence Avenue SE
Washington, DC 20540
202-707-5000
http://www.loc.gov
With 34,528,818 volumes on hand, the Library of Congress is the largest library in the United States. Visitors can browse the stacks of books, recordings, photographs, maps, manuscripts, films, and audio podcasts in the library's collections.

Source Notes

CHAPTER 1. DR. MAYA ANGELOU: LEGENDARY POET

1. "Remarks by the President Honoring the Recipients of the 2010 Medal of Freedom." *WhiteHouse.gov*. White House, 15 Feb. 2011. Web. 24 Sept. 2015.

2. Ibid.

3. Lindsay Deutsch. "13 of Maya Angelou's Best Quotes." *USA Today*. Gannett Company, 28 May 2014. Web. 24 Sept. 2015.

4. Emma Brown. "Maya Angelou, Writer and Poet, Dies at Age 86." *Washington Post*. Graham Holdings Company, 28 May 2014. Web. 24 Sept. 2015.

5. Sarah Loff, Ed. "Poem by American Matriarch Flown on Orion Presented to NASA Administrator." *NASA.gov*. National Aeronautics and Space Administration, 30 July 2015. Web. 24 Sept. 2015.

6. Alexandra Alter. "Remembrances: Author, Poet Maya Angelou Dies." *Wall Street Journal*. Dow Jones & Company, 28 May 2014. Web. 24 Sept. 2015.

CHAPTER 2. LITERARY FICTION

1. Amy Ahearn. "Willa Cather: Longer Biographical Sketch." *Willa Cather Archive*. Center for Research in the Humanities, University of Nebraska-Lincoln, n.d. Web. 2 Nov. 2015.

2. Johann Hari. "How Ayn Rand Became an American Icon." *Slate*. The Slate Group, 2 Nov. 2009. Web. 2 Nov. 2015.

3. Helen T. Verongos. "Doris Lessing, Author Who Swept Aside Convention, Is Dead at 94." *International New York Times*. New York Times Company, 17 Nov. 2013. Web. 2 Nov. 2015.

4. Ibid.

5. Ibid.

6. Elizabeth Day. "The 10 Best Short Story Collections." *Guardian*. Guardian News and Media Limited, 17 Oct. 2014. Web. 2 Nov. 2015.

7. Alison Flood. "Baileys Prize Crowns Chimamanda Ngozi Adichie as its 'Best of the Best.'" *Guardian*. Guardian News and Media Limited, 2 Nov. 2015. Web. 2 Nov. 2015.

CHAPTER 3. GENRE FICTION

1. Linda Wertheimer, Narr. "Author Jackie Collins Remembered for Impact on Steamy Fiction." *NPR: Weekend Edition Sunday*. National Public Radio, 20 Sept. 2015. Web. 2 Nov. 2015.

2. Petra Mayer, Narr. "Beverly Jenkins Wraps Bitter History in Sweet Romance." *NPR: Weekend Edition Sunday*. National Public Radio, 8 Aug. 2015. Web. 2 Nov. 2015.

3. Ibid.

4. Ibid.

5. Andrew Taylor. "Agatha Christie: The Curious Case of the Cosy Queen." *Independent*. Independent, 22 July 2010. Web. 15 Mar. 2016.

6. Diana Reese. "Blanche White, Maid Turned Sleuth in '90s Murder Mystery Series, Is Back." *Washington Post*. Nash Holdings, 3 Jan. 2015. Web. 2 Nov. 2015.

CHAPTER 4. SCIENCE FICTION

1. Cari Romm. "The Enduring Scariness of the Mad Scientist." *Atlantic*. Atlantic Monthly Group, 29 Oct. 2014. Web. 2 Nov. 2015.

2. Madeleine L'Engle. *A Circle of Quiet*. New York: HarperOne, 1984. Print.

3. Jennifer Maloney. "A New 'Wrinkle in Time.'" *Wall Street Journal*. Dow Jones & Company, 16 Apr. 2015. Web. 2 Nov. 2015.

4. Andrew Liptak. "The Left and Right Hands of Ursula K. Le Guin." *Kirkus Reviews*. Kirkus Media LLC, 14 Aug. 2014. Web. 2 Nov. 2015.

5. Julie Phillips. "The Real and Unreal: Ursula K. Le Guin, American Novelist." *Bookslut*. Bookslut, Dec. 2012. Web. 2 Nov. 2015.

CHAPTER 5. NONFICTION AND MEMOIR

1. Jinnie Lee and Maura M. Lynch. "11 Nonfiction Books That Deserve Your Attention." *Refinery29.com*. Refinery 29, 7 Oct. 2014. Web. 2 Nov. 2015.

2. David A. Fahrenthold. "'Mother' of Environmentalism Celebrated." *Washington Post*. Washington Post, 7 Mar. 2007. Web. 2 Nov. 2015.

3. Ibid.

4. Rebecca Solnit. "Tomgram: Rebecca Solnit, The Archipelago of Arrogance." *TomDispatch.com*. Rebecca Solnit, 13 Apr. 2008. Web. 15 Mar. 2016.

5. Jonathan Yardley. "'Woman Warrior,' A Memoir That Shook the Genre." *Washington Post*. Washington Post, 19 June 2007. Web. 2 Nov. 2015.

6. Dorothy Gallagher. "Making Ends Meet." *New York Times*. New York Times Company, 13 May 2001. Web. 2 Nov. 2015.

7. Rachel Syme. "10 of the Best 'Dear Sugar' Advice Columns by Wild Author Cheryl Strayed." *Vulture*. New York Media LLC., 23 Dec. 2014. Web 2 Nov. 2015.

8. Margalit Fox. "Pauline Phillips, Flinty Adviser to Millions as Dear Abby, Dies at 94." *International New York Times*. New York Times Company, 17 Jan. 2013. Web. 2 Nov. 2015.

CHAPTER 6. FEMINIST WRITING

1. John Lichfield. "Still the Second Sex? Simone de Beauvoir Centenary." *Independent*. Independent Print Limited, 22 Oct. 2011. Web. 2 Nov. 2015.

2. Betty Friedan. *The Feminine Mystique*. New York: Norton, 2010. Print. 133.

3. "History–Pen Women Then and Now." *National League of American Pen Women*. NLAPW, 2016. Web. 15 Mar. 2016.

4. "What Germaine Greer and The Female Eunuch Mean to Me." *Guardian*. Guardian News and Media Limited, 27 Jan. 2014. Web. 2 Nov. 2015.

5. Douglas Martin. "Flo Kennedy, Feminist, Civil Rights Advocate and Flamboyant Gadfly, Is Dead at 84." *New York Times*. New York Times Company, 23 Dec. 2000. Web. 2 Nov. 2015.

6. "Bell Hooks Biography." *Encyclopedia of World Biography*. Advameg, Inc., n.d. Web. 2 Nov. 2015.

Source Notes Continued

7. Roxane Gay. *Bad Feminist*. New York: HarperCollins, 2014. Print. xi.

CHAPTER 7. POETRY

1. "Emily Dickinson." *Poets.org*. Academy of the American Poets, n.d. Web. 2 Nov. 2015.

2. "Edna St. Vincent Millay." *Poetry*. Poetry Foundation, n.d. Web. 2 Nov. 2015.

3. "Anne Sexton." *Poetry*. Poetry Foundation, n.d. Web. 2 Nov. 2015.

4. Elizabeth Hardwick. "On Sylvia Plath." *New York Review of Books*. NYREV, Inc., 23 May 2013. Web. 2 Nov. 2015.

5. "Gwendolyn Brooks." *Poetry*. Poetry Foundation, n.d. Web. 2 Nov. 2015.

6. Elizabeth Ann Beaulieu. *Writing African American Women*. Westport, CT: Greenwood, 2006. Print. 365.

7. "Giovanni, Yolande Cornelia "Nikki" (1943-)." *BlackPast.org*. BlackPast.org, n.d. Web. 2 Nov. 2015.

8. "Sandra Cisneros Looks Back as a Writer in Search of Home." *PBS.org*. NewsHour Productions, 29 Oct. 2015. Web. 2 Nov. 2015.

9. Caroline Rothstein. "Slamming Barriers." *Narratively*. Narratively, n.d. Web. 2 Nov. 2015.

CHAPTER 8. YOUNG ADULT LITERATURE

1. Kathryn Zickuhr and Lee Rainie. "Younger Americans' Reading Habits and Technology Use." *PewResearchCenter*. Pew Research Center, 10 Sept. 2014. Web. 2 Nov. 2015.

2. Laura Stampler. "Adult Books Sales Are Down and Young Adult Soars in 2014." *Time*. Time Inc., 16 Dec. 2014. Web. 2 Nov. 2015.

3. Anna Richard. "Young Adult Books by the Numbers." *BloomingTwig.com*. Blooming Twig Books, 14 June 2014. Web. 2 Nov. 2015.

4. Margalit Fox. "Maureen Daly, 85, Chronicler of Teenage Love, Dies." *New York Times*. New York Times Company, 29 Sept. 2006. Web. 2 Nov. 2015.

5. Jon Michaud. "S.E. Hinton and the Y.A. Debate." *New Yorker*. Condé Nast, 14 Oct. 2014. Web. 2 Nov. 2015

6. Susan Dominus. "Judy Blume Knows All Your Secrets." *New York Times Magazine*. New York Times Company, 18 May 2015. Web. 2 Nov. 2015.

7. Ashley Strickland. "A Brief History of Young Adult Literature." *CNN.com*. Turner Broadcasting System, Inc., 15 Apr. 2015. Web. 2 Nov. 2015.

8. "Children's Books by and about People of Color and First/Native Nations Published in the United States." *CCBC*. Cooperative Children's Books Center, 24 Feb. 2015. Web. 2 Nov. 2015.

9. "Diversity Gap in Children's Publishing, 2015." *Lee & Low Books*. Lee & Low Books, 5 Mar. 2015. Web. 6 Mar. 2016.

10. Jacqueline Woodson. "The Pain of the Watermelon Joke." *New York Times*. New York Times Company, 28 Nov. 2014. Web. 2 Nov. 2015.

CHAPTER 9. TODAY'S LITERARY STARS

1. Roxane Gay. "Where Things Stand." *The Rumpus*. The Rumpus, 6 Jun. 2012. Web. 2 Nov. 2015.

2. Ibid.

3. Kyle Norris. "Comics Crusader: Remembering Jackie Ormes." *NPR: All Things Considered*. National Public Radio, 15 July 2011. Web. 2 Nov. 2015.

4. Erin Maxwell. "Women Quietly Become a Force in Comic Book World." *Variety*. Penske Business Media, LLC, 6 Oct. 2015. Web. 2 Nov. 2015.

5. Laura Sneddon. "Kate Beaton on Refusing to Let Women Be Forgotten and Increasing Audience Diversity of a Comic Convention." *Independent*. Independent, 2 Nov. 2015. Web. 2 Nov. 2015.

6. Lev Grossman. "Kate Beaton: How to Make It as a Cartoonist." *Time*. Time Inc., 7 July 2015. Web. 2 Nov. 2015.

7. Alexandra Alter. "Transgender Children's Books Fill a Void and Break a Taboo." *International New York Times*. New York Times Company, 6 June 2015. Web. 2 Nov. 2015.

8. Roxane Gay. "Roxane Gay Is Spelled with One 'N': Same Numbers, Different Year." *The Rumblr*. TheRumpus.net, 4 Mar. 2013. Web. 2 Nov. 2015.

Index

About the Author

Alexis Burling has written dozens of articles and books for young readers on a variety of topics, including current events and famous people, nutrition and fitness, careers and money management, relationships, and cooking. She is also a book critic (and obsessive reader) with reviews of both adult and young adult books, author interviews, and other industry-related articles published in the *New York Times*, the *Washington Post*, the *San Francisco Chronicle*, and more.